Fantasy
CAKES

Fantasy CAKES

Magical recipes
for fanciful bakes

ANGELA ROMEO

photography by
ADRIAN LAWRENCE

RYLAND PETERS & SMALL
LONDON • NEW YORK

For Giuseppe – my sweet, fellow maker.

A CIP record for this book is available from the British Library. US Library of Congress Cataloging-in-Publication Data has been applied for.

Notes:
- Both British (Metric) and American (Imperial plus US cups) measurements are included in these recipes for your convenience, however it is important to work with one set of measurements only and not alternate between the two within a recipe.
- All spoon measurements are level unless otherwise specified. A teaspoon is 5 ml, a tablespoon is 15 ml.
- All eggs are medium (UK) or large (US), unless specified as large, in which case US extra-large should be used. Uncooked or partially cooked eggs should not be served to the very old, frail, young children, pregnant women or those with compromised immune systems.
- Ovens should be preheated to the specified temperatures. We recommend using an oven thermometer. If using a fan-assisted oven, adjust temperatures according to the manufacturer's instructions.

Senior designer Toni Kay
Editors Alice Sambrook and Kate Eddison
Production controller David Hearn
Art director Leslie Harrington
Editorial director Julia Charles
Publisher Cindy Richards

Food stylist Angela Romeo
Prop stylist Olivia Wardle
Indexer Hilary Bird

First published in 2017 by
Ryland Peters & Small
20–21 Jockey's Fields, London WC1R 4BW
and 341 E 116th St, New York NY 10029
www.rylandpeters.com

10 9 8 7 6 5 4 3 2 1

Text copyright © Angela Romeo 2017
Design and photographs copyright
© Ryland Peters & Small 2017

ISBN: 978-1-84975-885-7

Printed in China

Contents

Introduction 6
Equipment 8
Techniques & Finishing Touches 10
Basic Recipes 14

Fruits & Flowers 24
Spectacular Celebrations 48
Candy Land 70
Psychedelic Treats 94
Magical Days Out 112
Decadent Divas 132

Index 156
Acknowledgements 160

INTRODUCTION

What other food out there do we adorn with ignited, flaming candles, enter into a room with, and present to an already delighted, singing audience?

The celebration cake holds a special place in my heart as a no-holds-barred edible blank canvas to get as creative as you like with. You can really let your imagination go wild.

Lots of us are afraid of cake decorating or are unsure where to start. In this book, I hope to show that by combining some basic techniques with clever easy-to-assemble toppings you can heighten the theatre without ramping up the dramas in the kitchen.

Sometimes simply using the right decoration to literally stick on top of a cake can turn the humble sponge into a masterpiece. I love to use time-saving readymade favourites in a different context to create show-stopping effects, from chocolate buttons as the centres of sunflowers to towers made of popcorn and mini doughnuts/donuts that make the most of a cakey stage.

There should be a cake for everyone in this collection of recipes and designs to suit different tastes and cake decorating abilities. There are more intricate toppers for those quiet moments when you have the time to enjoy modelling a handcrafted flower or a madhatter's teapot, but there are also plenty of striking designs that are much simpler to achieve than they look when life just gets too busy. Ssshhh we just won't tell anyone!

Get experimenting and adapt the designs to make them your own; this is the beauty of this type of cake decorating, there really aren't any rules – the most important thing is to enjoy getting creative and really don't worry if your sides aren't 'freshly-plastered' smooth or you've got a wonky drip. A few dents and scrapes isn't the end of the cakey world. Embrace the charm and scatter with more sprinkles!

EQUIPMENT

Surely I need lots of expensive decorating tools? You'll be surprised at the results you can achieve with a palette knife/metal spatula and dinner knife. I confess I'm not exactly a minimalist when it comes to cake decorating equipment – a miniature palette knife or Russian flower nozzle/tip can leave me weak at the knees, but these things aren't essential (and most of the time I can't remember where I've put them!). So here's a round-up of kit that will get you off to a flying, fantastical start.

CAKE PANS

Most of the larger cakes in this book use 18-cm/ 7-inch round cake pans (at least 4.5 cm/1¾ inches in height) or 20-cm/8-inch round deep cake pans. Three 18-cm/7-inch cakes sandwiched together create a tall and striking cake. If you have only two 18-cm/7-inch pans, the sponge mixture will hold well while the other sponges are baking, so you can bake in batches. Cover the remaining third of batter in clingfilm/plastic wrap, until ready to bake.

BAKING PARCHMENT

Don't forget the baking parchment! It's essential to grease and line cake pans, making it easy to release the cakes once they're baked.

COCKTAIL STICKS/TOOTHPICKS

Perfect for checking sponge in shallower cakes is cooked without creating a big hole. They are great for adding small amounts of colour to buttercream.

DINNER KNIFE

I apply the first layer of buttercream for the crumb coating with a dinner knife. Its ridged blade provides more control and it is harder to overload the knife.

PALETTE KNIFE/METAL SPATULA

A long palette knife/metal spatula is great for smoothing buttercream, helping to get both smooth sides and a flat top. An offset palette knife helps to get a flat top without the handle getting in the way.

DISPOSABLE PIPING/PASTRY BAGS

Disposable piping/pastry bags certainly make cake decorating life easier for obvious reasons, but they're also great if you haven't lots of nozzles/tips. Simply snip a small hole in the end to pipe fine lines (although you will have a little less control) and if making meringue kisses, simply snip a larger hole in the end. And even though technically they are disposable, don't forget you can wash them up, too!

PIPING NOZZLES/TIPS

Some packs of disposable piping/pastry bags include a basic set of nozzles/tips – these are great to get started with, and a small star nozzle/tip, a small round nozzle/tip and leaf nozzles/tips are often included in these packs. Master one technique with the relevant nozzle, and it can be an inexpensive way to create a truly dramatic effect.

WOODEN SKEWERS

From the base of a hard-boiled sweet/hard candy sparkler or the hidden structure inside an anti-gravity cake to marking guidance lines in buttercream – wooden skewers are great to have to hand in a cake decorator's kitchen.

FOOD COLOURING PASTES/GELS

To get vibrant buttercream colours, it's worth investing in a basic palette of food colouring pastes or gels. Powders or liquids can affect the consistency of buttercream or icing. Bright and dark colours are the most difficult to achieve but remember that buttercream tends to become a shade darker on standing. If you are looking to achieve a bright or dark colour when using sugarpaste, it is best to buy it readymade – it is readily available in most supermarkets.

TURNTABLE

Not 100% essential, but it certainly does make life easier, especially when removing excess buttercream and smoothing sides.

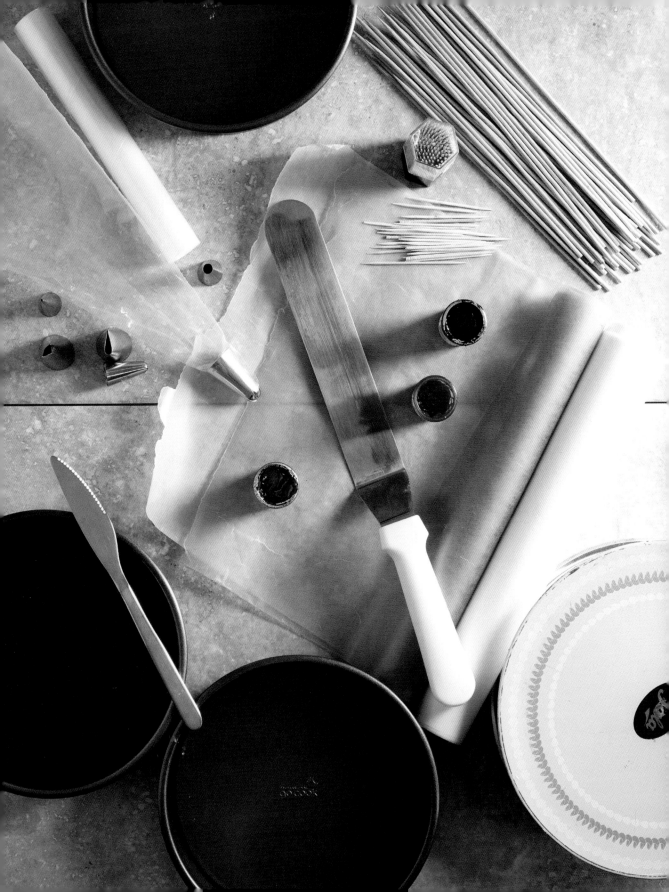

TECHNIQUES & FINISHING TOUCHES

LINING PANS

To line a round cake pan, grease the inside with butter or vegetable fat. Place the pan on a piece of baking parchment and draw round the base. Cut out the circle and use to line the round base. Cut a long strip of baking parchment, long enough to go around the circumference of the pan. Press onto the sides.

Top Tip: To save waste, you can line the sides with off-cuts from cutting out the round. Keep them all the same height but overlap slightly as you press them onto the sides.

My ultimate shortcut way to line a square pan is to grease the inside with butter or vegetable fat. Cut a wide strip of baking parchment so that it fits the width of the pan and comes up two of the sides. Grease the top of the paper in the base of the pan and repeat; lay the second strip on top of the first strip in the other direction so that it covers the unlined sides.

CRUMB-COATING

1 A spoonful of icing spread onto the middle of your cake board will stop your cake from moving around.
2 When crumb-coating it's best to apply the buttercream little and often, this will help to give an even distribution and prevent dragging crumbs around the cake. Use the tip of a dinner knife to apply icing to the sides and top of your stacked cake, slightly spreading a little more buttercream into any gaps or recesses, if necessary.
3 Smooth the top with a palette knife/metal spatula. At this stage, the sides do not need to be completely smooth.
4 When the cake is covered, take the palette knife/ metal spatula or a cake scraper and hold vertically at a 45° angle against the cake. Sweep around the cake with a little pressure to remove the excess icing. Scrape this icing into a separate bowl (as it may have crumbs in) and continue to remove the excess buttercream. If there are any gaps or holes,

fill with a little buttercream and smooth again with the palette knife/metal spatula or cake scraper.
5 After finishing the sides, you will have little peaks at the top edge of your cake, use the palette knife/ metal spatula, held horizontally, to draw these peaks into the centre of the cake, using gentle but sturdy sweeping motions. Chill the cake for 15 minutes.

FINAL COAT

After the cake has chilled, use the same technique as crumb-coating for the final coat. However, when using your palette knife/metal spatula or cake scraper to smooth the sides, apply slightly less pressure with a narrower angle – you want to aim to 'spread' the buttercream around the cake whilst maintaining the straight sides.

CLEVER COVER-UPS

Choose your cake carefully; if you want to practise your buttercream skills, choose a cake with chocolate bark or lots of detail on the sides. This will ensure you'll get a professional, impressive finish, enabling you to work up to cakes that show off completely smooth sides.

THE ULTIMATE DRIP

CHOCOLATE

To make the perfect drizzle using dark/bittersweet chocolate, ensure you use a brand with a minimum of 85% cocoa solids. When melted this will ensure a nice, runny, pourable consistency.

Candy Melts, milk chocolate or white chocolate may have a slightly thicker consistency after melting and may need thinning a little – after melting stir through a little vegetable fat, if necessary, such as Trex or Cookeen. Stir until fully melted; if there are still lumps gently heat again.

ICING

If drizzling with icing, I like to use royal icing rather than glacé icing. When thick, but fluid with a pourable consistency it enables good control if you want to aim a drip in a specific place!

FRUITY DRIPS

Fruit sauces are a great way to get dark drips using natural colour; reducing down a mixture of fruit, sugar and water on the hob is the simplest way to do this. The longer it bubbles away for, the thicker it will be. To thicken further, add a little arrowroot or cornflour/cornstarch.

BUTTERCREAM KNOW-HOW

There are lots of small tweaks and options when making buttercream. The cakes in this collection will advise on the buttercream used for that particular recipe, but the three main buttercream recipes in this book are interchangeable, so feel free to get experimenting and use your favourite:

THE CLASSIC

My classic buttercream (see page 20) has a mix of butter and vegetable fat. The vegetable fat helps to keep the buttercream stable – enabling it to hold its shape even in a warm climate. It also helps the buttercream form a crust, making it less sticky and more robust. Perfect for transporting to a party!

BRILLIANT WHITE

The brilliant white buttercream (see page 21) in this book is a perfect vegan option, using only vegetable fat, icing/confectioners' sugar and vanilla extract. On its own the vegetable fat will not form a crust like it does when mixed with butter, but it is great if you want a surface to stick decorations to.

TWO-INGREDIENT

I love whipping up a cake even when I haven't got much in the fridge or kitchen cupboards, so this one (see page 20) is for when inspiration strikes and you just want to get started!

WONDERS OF WATER

Lots of recipes will require you to add milk to buttercream to get a spreadable consistency; I prefer to use a little water. This way, a fully coated cake won't need to be stored in the fridge and at the same time the buttercream will keep the sponge airtight, so it will happily sit on the side in a cake box.

USE A FOOD PROCESSOR

This is a speedy shortcut. If you have a food processor, it's great to use to make short work of making buttercream. The blade is perfect for cutting through and blending, with the added bonus that there won't be any puffing clouds of icing/confectioners' sugar!

ALTERNATIVELY... BEAT IT

If you haven't got a food processor, beat the butter with an electric hand whisk or in a free-standing mixer until soft and pale. (Note, if you are making the vegan icing with a hand whisk, the vegetable fat at room temperature will be very soft, so there's no need to beat it first.) Add the vegetable fat (if using), the water and flavouring as advised in your recipe. Gradually whisk in the sifted icing/confectioners' sugar in batches (or you may find it easier to fold in the sugar manually first to avoid sugar clouds), then whisk through with the electric hand whisk. Whisk in a little more water if needed.

Traditional vanilla sponge

This all-in-one mix is a super speedy way
to a delicious classic cake base.

500 g /3¾ cups self-raising/
self-rising flour plus 1
teaspoon bicarbonate of
soda (omit soda if baking
with US flour), sifted

500 g/2½ cups caster/
superfine sugar

240 g/2¼ sticks butter, melted
and cooled, plus extra for
greasing

300 ml/1¼ cups buttermilk

4 eggs

1 teaspoon pure vanilla extract

**MAKES ENOUGH FOR
1 LARGE CAKE**

Preheat the oven to 180ºC (350ºF) Gas 4.
Place all the ingredients in a large bowl
and beat with an electric hand whisk until
combined and smooth. Transfer to greased
and lined pans specified in each recipe (if
using 18-cm/7-inch pans, ensure they are
at least 4.5 cm/1¾ inches deep and lined
with a 1.5-cm/²⁄₃-inch collar). Bake for the
time specified in each recipe.

Gluten-free vanilla sponge

Making sure no one misses out on cake with this moist gluten free sponge.

Preheat the oven to 180°C (350°F) Gas 4. Place the sugar and butter in a large bowl and beat with an electric hand whisk until pale and fluffy. Add all the remaining ingredients and beat until combined and smooth. Transfer to greased and lined pans specified in each recipe (if using 18-cm/ 7-inch pans, ensure they are at least 4.5 cm/1³/₄ inches deep and lined with a 1.5-cm/²/₃-inch collar). Bake for the time specified in each recipe.

450 g/2¹/₂ cups caster/ superfine sugar

450 g/4 sticks butter, softened, plus extra for greasing

450 g/scant 3¹/₂ cups gluten-free self-raising/ self-rising flour, sifted

8 eggs

1 teaspoon pure vanilla extract

75 ml/5 tablespoons milk

MAKES ENOUGH FOR 1 LARGE CAKE

Double chocolate sponge

Easiest ever deep, rich chocolate cake.

450 g/3½ scant cups self-raising/self-rising flour plus 2 teaspoons bicarbonate of soda, sifted (omit soda if baking with US flours)

3 tablespoons unsweetened cocoa powder, mixed with 4 tablespoons just-boiled water

500 g/2½ cups caster/superfine sugar

240 g/2¼ sticks butter, melted and cooled, plus extra for greasing

300 ml/1¼ cups buttermilk

4 eggs

1 teaspoon pure vanilla extract

150 g/5½ oz. dark/bittersweet chocolate, melted

MAKES ENOUGH FOR 1 LARGE CAKE

Preheat the oven to 180°C (350°F) Gas 4. Place all the ingredients in a large bowl and beat with an electric hand whisk until combined and smooth. Transfer to greased and lined pans specified in each recipe (if using 18-cm/7-inch cake pans, ensure they are at least 4.5 cm/1¾ inches deep and lined with a 1.5-cm/⅔-inch collar). Bake for the time specified in each recipe.

Gluten-free double chocolate sponge

This luscious chocolate cake is a great all-rounder. It also freezes well – freeze for up to 3 months.

Preheat the oven to 180°C (350°F) Gas 4. Place the sugar and butter in a large bowl and beat with an electric hand whisk until pale and fluffy. Add all the remaining ingredients and beat until combined. Transfer to greased and lined pans specified in each recipe (if using 18-cm/7-inch cake pans, ensure they are at least 4.5 cm/1¾ inches deep and lined with a 1.5-cm/²/₃-inch collar). Bake for the time specified in each recipe.

400 g/2 cups caster/superfine sugar

400 g/3½ sticks butter, plus extra for greasing

400 g/3 cups gluten-free self-raising/self-rising flour, sifted

3 tablespoons unsweetened cocoa powder, mixed with 4 tablespoons just-boiled water

150 g/5½ oz. dark/bittersweet chocolate, melted

8 eggs

1 teaspoon pure vanilla extract

MAKES ENOUGH FOR 1 LARGE CAKE

Dessert-style sponge

A versatile fat free springy sponge – the perfect base for showing off punchy and vibrant flavours.

6 UK large/US extra-large eggs, separated

200 g/1 cup caster/superfine sugar

2 teaspoons pure vanilla extract

200 g/1½ cups self-raising/self-rising flour, sifted (for chocolate dessert-style sponge, replace 50 g/6 tablespoons of the flour with 50 g/½ cup cocoa powder)

MAKES ENOUGH FOR 1 LARGE CAKE

Preheat the oven to 180ºC (350ºF) Gas 4. Whisk the egg whites to form stiff peaks. Gradually whisk in half the sugar until glossy.

In a separate bowl, beat the yolks and vanilla extract with the remaining sugar until thick and creamy. Sift in the flour (and cocoa powder if using), add the egg whites and fold all the ingredients together with a wooden spoon. Transfer to greased and lined pans specified in each recipe (if using 18-cm/7-inch cake pans, ensure they are at least 4.5 cm/1¾ inches deep and lined with a 1.5-cm/²/₃-inch collar). Bake for the time specified in each recipe.

Vegan chocolate sponge

No one will be able to refuse a slice of this lovely rich fudgy, chocolate cake.

Preheat the oven to 180°C (350°F) Gas 4. Place the banana in a large bowl and mash until creamy. Add the soya milk, vegetable oil, sugar, vanilla extract, white wine vinegar and maple syrup. Beat with an electric hand whisk until combined. Sift over the flour, cocoa powder and baking powder and fold through until combined. Transfer to greased and lined pans specified in each recipe (if using 18-cm/ 7-inch cake pans, ensure they are at least 4.5 cm/1³/₄ inches deep and lined with a 1.5-cm/²/₃-inch collar). Bake for the time specified in each recipe.

1 large ripe banana, 115 g/ 4 oz. peeled weight

250 ml/1 cup soya milk

75 ml/5 tablespoons vegetable oil

425 g/generous 2 cups caster/superfine sugar

2 teaspoons pure vanilla extract

2 teaspoons white wine vinegar

115 ml/scant ¹/₂ cup maple syrup

575 g/generous 4¹/₄ cups self-raising/self-rising flour, sifted

75 g/³/₄ cup unsweetened cocoa powder

1 tablespoon baking powder

MAKES ENOUGH FOR 1 LARGE CAKE

BASIC RECIPES: FROSTINGS

Classic buttercream

Great for both swirling on cupcakes and decorating big cakes. It keeps well, covered, in a cool place, out of the fridge, for up to 5 days.

Using an electric hand whisk, beat the butter until light and creamy. Add the vegetable fat, vanilla and 2 tablespoons water. Gradually whisk in the icing/confectioners' sugar in batches, until smooth and spreadable. Add another 1 tablespoon water, if needed.

300 g/2¾ sticks butter, softened and cubed

200 g/7 oz. vegetable fat such as Trex or Cookeen, at room temperature

2 teaspoons pure vanilla extract

1 kg/7 cups icing/confectioners' sugar, sifted

MAKES 1.5 KG/3 LB. 5 OZ.

Two-ingredient buttercream

An easy recipe to keep in mind when inspiration strikes, or if you want to make up a small batch of buttercream to add individual touches. Simply remember 1 part butter to 2 parts icing/confectioners' sugar.

Using an electric hand whisk, beat the butter until light and creamy. Add 2 tablespoons water and gradually whisk in the icing/confectioners' sugar in manageable batches, until smooth and spreadable. Add another 1 tablespoon of water if necessary.

500 g/4½ sticks butter, softened and cubed

1 kg/7 cups icing/confectioners' sugar, sifted

MAKES 1.5 KG/3 LB. 5 OZ.

Brilliant white buttercream (vegan)

Not only the perfect vegan choice, the bright white colour of this buttercream means you can create really striking results when an icy white base is needed.

500 g/1 lb. 2 oz. vegetable fat such as Trex or Cookeen, at room temperature

1 kg/7 cups icing/confectioners' sugar, sifted

2 teaspoons pure vanilla extract

MAKES 1.5 KG/3 LB. 5 OZ.

Place the vegetable fat in a bowl with the vanilla extract, 2 tablespoons water and a few large spoonfuls of the icing/confectioners' sugar. Whisk with an electric hand whisk until combined, then whisk in the remaining icing/confectioners' sugar in manageable batches, until smooth and spreadable. Add another 1 tablespoon of water, if necessary.

Speedy shortcut:

If you have a food processor, blending buttercream couldn't be simpler, for Classic Buttercream and Two-ingredient Buttercream, process the butter until light and creamy. Add the remaining ingredient(s) with 2 tablespoons of water and blend until smooth with a good spreadable consistency. Add another 1 tablespoon of water if necessary. For the Brilliant White Buttercream, whizz all the ingredients together until smooth and creamy. Add another 1 tablespoon of water if necessary.

Royal icing

Royal icing for big cakes gets a bit of a modern makeover, gone are snow-scene-style peaks, by keeping it a little more fluid it's the perfect choice for dazzling drips.

2 UK large/US extra-large egg whites

250 g/1¾ cups icing/confectioners' sugar, sifted

½ teaspoon glycerine

MAKES ENOUGH TO TOP AND DECORATE 1 LARGE CAKE

Place the egg whites in a bowl and whisk until frothy. Gradually add the sugar a spoonful at a time, while whisking, then continue to whisk for 3–5 minutes until the icing holds soft peaks. Stir through the glycerine (you can still get the same effect without glycerine – the glycerine just stops the icing setting quite so hard). Add a little water as specified in each recipe if needed.

Glossy black fudge icing

A sophisticated cake covering for creating
a dramatic statement.

Place the butter, sugar, cocoa powder, buttermilk and vanilla
extract in a food processor and pulse until combined. Add
the melted chocolate and pulse until smooth. Transfer to a
large bowl and stir through enough food colouring until you
get a dark brown-black colour. Remember it will darken on
standing. Allow to sit for 20 minutes, add more colouring
if necessary. Use immediately or set aside in a cool, dry
place, covered, until needed.

425 g/4 sticks butter,
softened

425 g/3 cups icing/
confectioners'
sugar, sifted

75 g/³⁄₄ cup
unsweetened dark
cocoa powder

90 ml/6 tablespoons
buttermilk

2 teaspoons pure
vanilla extract

225 g/8 oz. dark/
bittersweet
chocolate, melted

super black paste food
colouring

**MAKES ENOUGH
TO COAT 1
LARGE CAKE**

FRUITS & FLOWERS

Blueberry blues

Just when you thought blueberry cheesecake couldn't get any better...

975 g/7³/₄ cups blueberries (see cook's tip)

1 quantity of Traditional Vanilla Sponge mixture (see page 14)

100 g/¹/₂ cup caster/superfine sugar

2 teaspoons arrowroot powder

50 g/2 oz. digestive biscuits/graham crackers, crushed

20 g/1¹/₂ tablespoons butter, melted

400 g/scant 3 cups icing/confectioners' sugar, sifted

800 g/3¹/₂ cups mascarpone

3 18-cm/7-inch cake pans, greased and lined

SERVES 30

Preheat the oven to 180°C (350°F) Gas 4.

Stir 350 g/generous 3 cups of the blueberries through the batter. Divide the mixture between the three cake pans. Bake for 45–50 minutes until an inserted cocktail stick/toothpick comes out clean. Allow to cool in the pans for 10 minutes, then remove and place on a wire rack to cool completely. If necessary, trim the tops of the cakes to make level.

For the blueberry saucy-compote, place 300 g/scant 3 cups blueberries in a saucepan with 150 ml/²/₃ cup water and the caster/superfine sugar. Heat, stirring occasionally, for around 5 minutes, until the blueberries start to break. Mix the arrowroot powder with 1 tablespoon of water and add to the pan. Simmer for around 5–10 minutes until thickened and syrupy. Remove from the heat and allow to cool (it will thicken further on standing). Stir occasionally to prevent a skin from forming.

Stir the digestive biscuits/graham crackers into the melted butter and allow to cool.

To make the cheesecake frosting, beat the icing/confectioners' sugar into the mascarpone in manageable batches, with an electric hand whisk until smooth. Sandwich the cakes together using 400 g/14 oz. of the frosting – the bottom side of the top cake should be facing up. Place the cake on a serving plate or cake board. Use the remaining frosting to coat the cake in a thick even layer. Smooth and remove any excess frosting with a palette knife/metal spatula.

Break up the cooled biscuits/crackers with a wooden spoon, if necessary, then gently press the crumbs around the bottom of the cake to resemble the base of a cheesecake. Chill until ready to serve.

When ready to serve, pile the remaining fresh blueberries on the top of the cake, then spoon over the cooled saucy-compote.

Cook's tip:
You could replace 300 g/scant 3 cups of the fresh blueberries with frozen blueberries for the saucy-compote (reduce the water to 100 ml/¹/₃ cup).

For gluten-free:
Use 1 quantity of Gluten-free Vanilla Sponge mixture (see page 15) and gluten-free digestive biscuits/graham crackers. Follow the recipe above and bake the cakes for 45–50 minutes, until an inserted cocktail stick/toothpick comes out clean.

Pineapple passion

Retro gold pineapple anyone? This chocolate and pineapple combo is a match made in heaven.

432-g/15-oz or 16-oz can pineapple chunks in juice, drained, puréed until mainly smooth but with a little texture

½ quantity of Traditional Vanilla Sponge mixture (see page 14)

75 g/¾ cup ground almonds

250 g/9 oz. dark/bittersweet chocolate, minimum 70% cocoa solids, melted

50 g/3½ tablespoons butter, softened

100 g/¾ cup icing/confectioners' sugar, sifted

2 egg whites

⅛ teaspoon cream of tartar

150 g/¾ cup caster/superfine sugar

2 tablespoons unsweetened cocoa powder

edible gold spray

2 500-ml/2-cup round Pyrex bowls, greased with sunflower oil and each base-lined with a 9-cm/3½-inch disc of baking parchment

piping/pastry bag fitted with a small round nozzle/tip

piping/pastry bag fitted with a 15-mm/⅝-inch nozzle

cook's blowtorch

SERVES 14

Preheat the oven to 180°C (350°F) Gas 4.

Stir the puréed pineapple through the cake batter along with the ground almonds. Divide the mixture between the two Pyrex bowls (leave a 2-cm/¾-inch gap at the top of each bowl). Bake for 45–50 minutes until an inserted skewer comes out clean. Leave to cool in the bowls for 20 minutes. Loosen the sides with a palette knife/metal spatula, invert onto a wire rack to cool completely, then chill for at least 1 hour. If necessary, trim the tops of the cakes to make level.

Meanwhile, make the chocolate palms. Draw about eight palm-shapes in various lengths from 10–24 cm/4–9½ inches on a piece of baking parchment. Lay the baking parchment on a large baking sheet (turn over so the pencil is on the underside). Draw five 5-cm/2-inch pointed finger shapes, side by side, onto a strip of baking parchment (turn over so the pencil is on the underside). Lay next to a rolling pin on a baking sheet.

Fill the piping/pastry bag fitted with a small round nozzle/tip with the melted chocolate. Working quickly, pipe around the palm shapes, then fill in the outlines with the chocolate, wiggling the parchment to level and fill any holes. Repeat with the finger shapes but drape over the rolling pin. Chill to set.

For the buttercream filling, whisk the butter until pale and creamy, then beat in the icing/confectioners' sugar with 1 teaspoon of water until smooth. Sandwich the two cakes together using most of buttercream. Use a little of the remaining buttercream to secure the base of the sponge on a heatproof cake board. Spread the flat top of the cake with the remaining buttercream. To make it easier to push the chocolate palms into the top of the cake, use a small, sharp, serrated knife to make slim indentations in the top of the cake.

For the meringue, using an electric hand whisk, whisk the egg whites with the cream of tartar until soft peaks form. Add the caster/superfine sugar and whisk for 5–8 minutes until stiff and glossy. Sift in the cocoa powder and fold through. Use to fill the piping/pastry bag fitted with a 15-mm/⅝-inch nozzle. Starting from the base, pipe small blobs of meringue, row by row, leaving the top of the cake exposed. Use a blowtorch to crisp the meringue.

Cover the edges of the cake board with baking parchment to protect it. Insert the central chocolate palm shapes into the top of the cake and spray gold. Add the outer palms and spray gold, then add the bent chocolate pieces around the base of the palm shapes and spray gold. Finally, spray the entire cake gold. Remove the baking parchment and serve.

Watermelon wonder

pink gel or paste food colouring

red gel or paste food colouring

1½ quantities of Traditional Vanilla Sponge mixture (see page 14)

75 g/2½ oz. plain/semisweet chocolate chips

1.95 kg/4 lb. 5 oz. Two-ingredient Buttercream (see page 20 using quantities 650 g/5⅔ sticks butter, 1.3 kg/9¼ cups icing/confectioners' sugar and 3–4 tablespoons water)

green gel or paste food colouring

black gel or paste food colouring

1 giant chocolate button

2-litre/2-quart/4-cup round Pyrex bowl, greased with sunflower oil and base-lined with a 10-cm/4-inch disc of baking parchment

2 20-cm/8-inch cake pans, greased and lined

flexible buttercream scraper

SERVES 30

Preheat the oven to 180°C (350°F) Gas 4.

Add enough pink and red food colouring to get a bright watermelon flesh-colour to the vanilla sponge mixture. Stir through the chocolate chips.

Pour 1.2 kg/2 lb. 11 oz. of the cake mixture into the prepared Pyrex bowl. Bring a double layer of baking parchment up and around the outside of the bowl, securing in place with kitchen string/twine.

Divide the remaining mixture between the prepared cake pans. Cover with a clean, damp kitchen towel and set aside.

Bake the cake in the Pyrex bowl for 1 hour 20–25 minutes until an inserted skewer comes out clean (after 45 minutes cover the top with a double layer of kitchen foil, and add the cake pans to the oven and bake for 35–40 minutes). Leave the cakes to cool in their pans for 10 minutes, then remove and allow to cool completely on a wire rack. Allow the cake in the bowl to cool for 30 minutes. Loosen the sides with a palette knife/metal spatula and invert onto a wire rack to cool completely.

Trim the tops of the flat cakes to make level. Stack the cakes so the domed cake is on the top. If necessary, trim the sides of the base cakes so they are flush with the domed cake. Colour 400 g/14 oz. of the buttercream the same watermelon flesh-colour as the cakes using the pink and red food colourings and use to sandwich the cakes together.

Crumb-coat the cake (see page 11) using 500 g/1 lb. 2 oz. of the white buttercream. The flexible buttercream scraper will help to smooth the icing over the rounded dome. Place in the freezer to harden for 15 minutes. With damp hands smooth down the buttercream a little more. Repeat using 450 g/1 lb. more of the white buttercream. Smooth down again with damp hands and return to the freezer for 15 minutes.

Colour the remaining 600 g/1 lb. 5 oz. of buttercream a light green shade. Use the same technique to coat the cake using 500 g/1 lb. 2 oz. of the green buttercream. Return to the freezer for 15 minutes. Add more green colouring and a little black colouring to get a mid-dark green shade to the remaining 100 g/3 oz. of buttercream. Use the tip of a dinner knife to apply the darker green buttercream smearing it downwards in small motions to create vertical stripes around the cake. Place in the freezer for 15 minutes. Smooth down again with damp hands, then top with a giant chocolate button and serve.

Citrus sensation

With such a zingy, refreshing flavour this zesty little number almost feels like a healthier cake option… I did say, almost!

1 quantity of Traditional Vanilla Sponge mixture (see page 14), mixed with the grated zest of 4 lemons, baked in three greased and lined 18-cm/7-inch cake pans for 35–40 minutes until an inserted cocktail stick/toothpick comes out clean; leave to cool in the pans for 10 minutes, but do not cool completely

For the lemon drizzle

freshly squeezed juice of 2 lemons

125 g/generous ¾ cup icing/confectioners' sugar, sifted

For the decoration

200 g/1 cup caster/superfine sugar, plus extra for sprinkling

2 lemons, thinly sliced and deseeded

zest of 1 lemon, pared with a vegetable peeler, then cut into thin long strips

2 tablespoons lemon curd

lemon thyme, to decorate

For the buttercream

275 g/2½ sticks butter

550 g/scant 4 cups icing/confectioners' sugar

2–3 tablespoons freshly squeezed lemon juice

disposable piping/pastry bag fitted with a large star nozzle/tip

SERVES 24

For the drizzle, mix the lemon juice and icing/confectioners' sugar. Use a skewer to poke deep holes into the cakes while they are still warm and in their pans. Pour over the drizzle (don't worry if it gathers at the edges, it will eventually soak in), then leave the cakes to cool completely in the pans.

Meanwhile, make the candied lemons and candied lemon spirals for decoration. In a saucepan, combine the sugar with 250 ml/1 cup water. Bring to the boil over a medium-high heat, stirring until the sugar dissolves. Add the lemon slices and pared lemon strips and simmer for 5–6 minutes until the pith of the lemon becomes semi-translucent. Using a slotted spoon, transfer to a wire rack set over a baking sheet to cool. Discard the syrup. When the pared strips are cool enough to handle, wind longer strips around cocktail sticks/toothpicks to create a spiral effect. Sprinkle with caster/superfine sugar and allow to set and cool completely.

For the buttercream, whisk the butter with an electric hand whisk (or in a food processor) until light and creamy. Add the icing/confectioners' sugar with 2 tablespoons of lemon juice and blend until smooth with a good spreadable consistency. If necessary, add another 1 tablespoon of lemon juice and 1 tablespoon of water.

If necessary, trim the tops of the cakes to make level. Reserve 150 g/5 oz. of the buttercream. Sandwich the cakes together using 350 g/12 oz. of the buttercream – the bottom side of the top cake should be facing up. Place the cake on a serving plate or cake board. Use the remainder to crumb-coat (see page 11) the cake – for this semi-naked effect, this will be your final coat, so be sure to scrape off enough of the buttercream to reveal the sponge underneath.

Stir the lemon curd through the reserved buttercream. Use to fill the piping/pastry bag fitted with the large star nozzle/tip. Pipe small swirls of the lemon curd buttercream on the top of the cake. Decorate the top and sides with the candied lemon slices and spirals, then scatter over a little lemon thyme.

For gluten-free:
Use 1 quantity of Gluten-free Vanilla Sponge mixture (see page 15) baked in three 18-cm/7-inch cake pans for 35–40 minutes. Leave to cool in the pans for 10 minutes, but do not cool completely.

1 quantity of Vegan Chocolate
   Sponge mixture (see page 19)
   baked in three greased and
   lined 18-cm/7-inch cake pans
   for 30–35 minutes until an
   inserted cocktail stick/
   toothpick comes out clean,
   then cooled

For the avocado frosting

2 ripe avocados, peeled, stoned/
   pitted and roughly chopped

75 g/2½ oz. vegetable fat, at
   room temperature, cubed

2 tablespoons freshly squeezed
   lemon juice

375 g/2⅔ cups icing/
   confectioners' sugar, sifted

2 teaspoons pure vanilla extract

For the decoration

2 food-safe, pesticide-free white
   roses

1 food-safe, pesticide-free pink
   rose, petals separated

3–5 raspberries

edible gold spray (optional)

1 cherry

food-safe gold glitter dust
   (optional)

1 teaspoon chopped pistachio
   nuts

1 teaspoon freeze-dried
   raspberries

SERVES 20

Avocado love

Vegan diet or not, this striking rich and moist cake with
a refreshing citrusy, avocado twist is a real crowd-pleaser.

For the avocado frosting, place all the frosting ingredients in a food
processor. Pulse until smooth. Chill for 1 hour before spreading.

Trim the tops of the cakes to make level – this will also make the frosting
grip the cake sufficiently, as its glossy nature means you need to use a
delicate hand when stacking and icing the cakes. On a cake board or
serving plate, carefully sandwich the cakes together using approximately
half of the frosting – the bottom side of the top cake should be facing up.

Crumb-coat (see page 11) the cake using the remaining frosting. This will
be your final coating giving it a semi-naked look, so be sure to scrape off
enough frosting to reveal some of the sponge. However, leave the coating
on the top a little thicker so that the decoration really stands out.

To decorate, place the roses, rose petals and raspberries to one side of
the top of the cake. Spray with a little edible gold spray, if using. Spray one
side of the cherry with a little edible gold spray, if using, then dip it in the
food-safe glitter dust, if using. Position amongst the flowers. Scatter the
chopped pistachio nuts and freeze-dried raspberries on the opposite side.

Using flowers and petals:

Use food-safe, pesticide-free flowers and petals only for decorating cakes.
Flowers are for decoration only and should be removed before cutting into
the cake. Pollen is allergenic and should not touch food. Only petals sold
as edible should be eaten. Never eat any floral decoration unless you are
certain it is safe to do so.

Raspberry ripple arctic tower cake

This is my modern take on that British classic, arctic roll. The key to this is to have all the elements ready, then when ready to serve, build it, run it to the table and watch it disappear!

1 quantity of Dessert-style Sponge mixture (see page 18) baked in three greased and lined 18-cm/7-inch cake pans for 20 minutes, then cooled

750 ml/3 cups good-quality vanilla ice cream

250 g/scant 2 cups raspberries, finely crushed, plus an extra 100 g/²/₃ cup to decorate

6 tablespoons seedless raspberry jam/jelly

For the raspberry sauce

40 g/3¹/₄ tablespoons caster/ superfine sugar

175 g/scant 1¹/₄ cups frozen raspberries

1 tablespoon freshly squeezed lemon juice

2 teaspoons arrowroot powder, mixed with 1 tablespoon water

For the white chocolate shards

150 g/5 oz. white chocolate

1 tablespoon freeze-dried raspberries

1 tablespoon strawberry crunch

2 baking sheets lined with baking parchment

SERVES 16

For the raspberry sauce, place the sugar, frozen raspberries and lemon juice in a saucepan and cook over a gentle heat, stirring, until the raspberries break down and the sugar has dissolved, about 3–5 minutes. Pass through a sieve/ strainer to remove the seeds. Return the sauce to the pan with the arrowroot mix. Stir over a gentle heat until thickened and syrupy. Allow to cool (it will thicken further on standing). Stir occasionally to prevent a skin from forming.

For the white chocolate shards, melt the white chocolate in a heatproof bowl set over a pan of simmering water (or microwave on high in 30-second bursts, stirring in between). Pour the melted white chocolate over one of the lined baking sheets and spread out to an approximate 18-cm/7-inch square. Before it sets completely, scatter with the freeze-dried raspberries and strawberry crunch. Freeze to set completely. Break into shards. Chill until needed.

Allow the ice cream to soften at room temperature for 30 minutes. Transfer to a large bowl, spoon over the crushed raspberries and 'cut through' the ice cream with a knife to distribute. Drizzle with 3 tablespoons of the raspberry sauce as you go (stir through a touch of water if it has thickened too much on standing). Transfer the bowl to the freezer and allow to firm up for another 1 hour. Scoop the ice cream into small balls on the second lined baking sheet. Freeze until ready to serve.

If necessary, trim the tops of the cakes to make level. When ready to serve, spread the tops of sponges with the jam/jelly – the bottom side of the top cake should be facing up. Place the base cake on a plate or cake board.

Sandwich the layers together using the scoops of ice cream. Finish with a layer of ice cream, then scatter over the extra raspberries and insert the white chocolate shards into the top. Drizzle with the remaining raspberry sauce.

Fig and pistachio cupcakes

The charm of Southern Italy in autumn on a cupcake – rich fresh figs, golden honey and sweetened mascarpone. A cheeky sprinkle of white sugar pearls gives a little nod to our September wedding in glorious Pollino National Park, Calabria.

50 g/generous ⅓ cup pistachio nuts, chopped, plus extra to decorate

½ quantity of Double Chocolate Sponge mixture (see page 16)

4 tablespoons runny honey, plus extra for brushing

525 g/2⅓ cups mascarpone

275 g/2 cups icing/confectioners' sugar

purple gel or paste food colouring

375 g/3¼ cups Nutella

6 figs, halved

1 teaspoon white sugar pearls

4 sheets edible gold leaf (optional)

12-hole muffin pan lined with paper cases

3 small disposable piping/pastry bags

large disposable piping/pastry bag fitted with a large star nozzle/tip

soft paintbrush

MAKES 12

Preheat the oven to 180°C (350°F) Gas 4.

Stir the pistachio nuts through the chocolate sponge mixture, then divide the mixture between the paper cases and bake in the preheated oven for 25 minutes, until an inserted cocktail stick/toothpick comes out clean. Allow to cool in the pan for 10 minutes, then transfer to a wire rack to cool completely. Brush the tops of the cakes with a little honey.

Whisk the mascarpone with the icing/confectioners' sugar and divide between two bowls. Stir the purple colouring through one of the bowls to get a mid-shade. Fill one small piping/pastry bag with the white frosting and one with the purple frosting. Mix the Nutella to loosen and use to fill the third small bag. Snip a 1.5-cm/½-inch hole from the end of each and place inside the large disposable piping/pastry bag fitted with a large star nozzle/tip.

Twist the top of the piping/pastry bag and pipe a swirl on the top of each cake. Decorate each with a fig half, some chopped pistachio nuts and white sugar pearls, then use a soft paintbrush to apply a little gold leaf to each fig, if using. Drizzle with the honey.

Ombre two-tier rose cake

½ quantity of Traditional Vanilla Sponge mixture (see page 14) baked in two greased and lined 18-cm/7-inch cake pans for 25–30 minutes until an inserted cocktail stick/toothpick comes out clean, then cooled

1 quantity of Traditional Vanilla Sponge mixture (see page 14) baked in two greased and lined deep 20-cm/8-inch cake pans for 45–50 minutes until an inserted cocktail stick/toothpick comes out clean, then cooled

2 quantities of Classic Buttercream (see page 20; you may find it easier to make this in two batches)

pink gel or paste food colouring

thin 18-cm/7-inch cake board

3 cake dowels

4 disposable piping/pastry bags

2d Wilton nozzle/tip (or a medium curved 6 pointed star-shaped nozzle/tip)

SERVES 30

If necessary, trim the tops of the cakes to make level. Use 175 g/6 oz. of the buttercream to sandwich the two 18-cm/7-inch cakes together. Place on the thin 18-cm/7-inch cake board.

Sandwich the two 20-cm/8-inch cakes together using 250 g/9 oz. of the buttercream and place on a separate cake board or plate. Place 950 g/2 lb. 2 oz. of the buttercream in a bowl, add enough pink colouring to get a pale pink shade and use to coat the cakes in a thick crumb coat (see page 11). Coat them separately as though you are making two cakes. Cut the dowels to the height of the larger cake and push into the centre of the cake in a triangle shape. Chill the cakes for 15 minutes.

Meanwhile, place 400 g/14 oz. of the remaining buttercream into a bowl and mix in enough of the food colouring to colour it a dark pink shade. Place another 400 g/14 oz. into another bowl and mix in enough of the food colouring to colour it a mid-pink shade. Place 300 g/10½ oz. buttercream into a third bowl and mix in enough food colouring to get a slightly lighter shade. Place the remaining 500 g/1 lb. 2 oz. in a bowl and mix in enough pink colouring to get the palest shade of pink.

Place the smaller cake on top of the larger cake. Fit one of the piping/pastry bags with the 2d Wilton nozzle/tip and fill with the darkest shade of pink. Starting at the base, pipe a single layer of swirls around the sides of the cake creating a ring of rose shapes. As the rose shapes are rounded, you may find you have a few small gaps, fill any gaps, as desired, with a little squeeze of buttercream to create small star-shapes. Repeat with the mid-shade of pink, using another piping/pastry bag fitted with the cleaned nozzle/tip, creating another ring of rose shapes that sit on top of the dark shade. Repeat with the slighter lighter shade creating a single layer on the smaller cake. Repeat with the palest shade of pink. Now the sides of the cake should be completely covered with rose shapes.

Pipe approximately seven roses around the edge on top of the cake in the palest shade, then pipe a larger rose to fill the centre.

For gluten-free:
Use ½ quantity of Gluten-free Vanilla Sponge mixture (see page 15) baked in two 18-cm/7-inch cake pans for 25–30 minutes until an inserted cocktail stick/toothpick comes out clean, and 1 quantity of Gluten-free Vanilla Sponge mixture (see page 15) baked in two deep 20-cm/8-inch cake pans for 45–50 minutes, until an inserted cocktail stick/toothpick comes out clean.

Sunflower cake

Sunflowers make me smile, a great cake to make for those sunny, happy people in life.

edible green paint (optional)

100 g/³/₄ cup sunflower seeds, toasted

1 quantity of Traditional Vanilla Sponge mixture (see page 14)

1.95 kg/4 lb. 5 oz. Two-ingredient Buttercream (see page 20, using quantities 650 g/5²/₃ sticks butter, 1.3 kg/9¹/₄ cups icing/confectioners' sugar and 3–4 tablespoons water)

blue, yellow and green gel or paste food colouring

350 g/12 oz. Nutella

icing/confectioners' sugar, for dusting

75 g/2¹/₂ oz. yellow flower modelling paste

1 tablespoon piping gel

20 giant chocolate buttons

16 standard-sized chocolate buttons

18–20 cocktail sticks/toothpicks

3 18-cm/7-inch cake pans, greased and lined

8-cm/3¹/₄-inch pastry/cookie cutter

3 disposable piping/pastry bags

Wilton 366 leaf nozzle/tip

small star nozzle/tip

5-cm/2-inch sunflower plunger cutter

3-cm/1¹/₄-inch sunflower plunger cutter

SERVES 20

Paint the cocktail sticks/toothpicks with edible green paint, if using. Leave to dry overnight.

Preheat the oven to 180°C (350°F) Gas 4.

Stir the sunflower seeds through the batter. Divide the mixture between the three cake pans. Bake for 35–40 minutes until an inserted cocktail stick/toothpick comes out clean. Allow to cool in the pans for 10 minutes, then remove and place on a wire rack to cool completely.

If necessary, trim the tops of the cakes to make level. Sandwich together using 350 g/12 oz. of the buttercream – the bottom side of the top cake should be facing up. Place on a serving plate and crumb-coat (see page 11) the cake using 450 g/1 lb. of the buttercream. Chill in the fridge for 15 minutes.

Place 550 g/1 lb. 3 oz. of the buttercream in a bowl and colour it blue. Use to coat the cake in a second layer of buttercream. Smooth and remove the excess buttercream with a palette knife/metal spatula.

Use 75 g/2¹/₂ oz. of the remaining buttercream to smear white blobs around the cake. Smooth and remove the excess buttercream to get a cloud effect. Use the 8-cm/3¹/₄-inch cutter to mark five round circles into the sides of the cake – space at different heights – so some may not be complete circles.

Colour 375 g/13 oz. of the remaining buttercream yellow. Fill a piping/pastry bag fitted with the leaf nozzle/tip and pipe petal shapes around the circles.

Fill a piping/pastry bag fitted with the small star nozzle/tip with the Nutella. Pipe small blobs to fill the circles, starting from the edges and working in.

Colour the remaining buttercream green and fill the third piping/pastry bag fitted with the cleaned star nozzle/tip. Pipe in clusters on the top of the cake.

On a work surface lightly dusted with icing/confectioners' sugar, roll out the yellow flower modelling paste to approximately 1 mm/¹/₁₆ inch thick. Use the plunger cutters to stamp out about ten large sunflower shapes and eight smaller sunflower shapes.

Working on one sunflower at a time, lay a cocktail stick/toothpick on top, gently pressing it slightly into the modelling paste. Brush the middle with the piping gel and stick the corresponding size chocolate button on top. Turn over, brush the back with piping gel and gently press on another chocolate button. Insert into the top of the cake to decorate and dry. Repeat with the remaining flower shapes.

Hello petal!

1 quantity of Traditional Vanilla Sponge mixture (see page 14) baked in three greased and lined 18-cm/7-inch cake pans for 35–40 minutes until an inserted cocktail stick/toothpick comes out clean, then cooled

1 quantity of Classic Buttercream (see page 20)

food-safe, pesticide-free coloured violas and pansies, to decorate

disposable piping/pastry bag fitted with an 8-mm/³⁄₈-inch round nozzle/tip

SERVES 20

Trim the tops of the cakes to make level, if necessary. Sandwich together using 350 g/12 oz. of the buttercream – the bottom side of the top cake should be facing up. Place the cake on a large cake board with a little buttercream underneath to keep the cake stable when you cut it in half.

Crumb-coat (see page 11) the cake using 400 g/14 oz. of the buttercream. Cut down the middle and prise apart to make two semi-circle cakes. Clean up any smeared buttercream from where the cakes have been pulled apart.

Reserve 100 g/3½ oz. of the buttercream. Crumb-coat the cut sides with some of the remaining buttercream. Place in the fridge for 15 minutes.

Coat the top and curved sides of the cake in a second layer using the remaining buttercream. Put the reserved buttercream in the piping/pastry bag fitted with the round nozzle/tip and twist the top. Working on the 'cut sides' of the cakes, pipe a line of buttercream along the very top and down the sides of the two outer edges – these buttercream borders will help to neatly contain the flowers within the 'cut-side' of the cake, adding to the dramatic effect. Use a small palette knife/metal spatula to smooth and integrate the piped borders with the rest of the buttercream, then smooth the curved sides and top of the cake further with a long palette knife/metal spatula or buttercream smoother.

Up to an hour before serving, gently press the flowers onto the 'cut sides' of the cake (if the buttercream has formed a seal by the time you serve, brush with a little water or edible glue). The flowers are for decorative purposes only and should be removed as you cut the cake.

For gluten-free:
1 quantity Gluten-free Vanilla Sponge mixture (see page 15) baked in three 18-cm/7-inch cake pans for 35–40 minutes, until an inserted cocktail stick/toothpick comes out clean.

For vegan:
1 quantity Vegan Chocolate Sponge mixture (see page 19) baked in three 18-cm/7-inch cake pans for 30–35 minutes, until an inserted cocktail stick/toothpick comes out clean. Allow the cakes to cool and use with 1 quantity Brilliant White Buttercream (see page 21).

Using flowers and petals:
See note on page 34.

Cake pop bouquet

Adding a touch of fresh mint to these rose cake pops really adds a realistic touch; wrap in cellophane for the ultimate edible Valentine's gift.

75 g/¾ stick butter, softened

75 g/6 tablespoons caster/ superfine sugar

1 egg

1 teaspoon pure vanilla extract

75 g/generous ½ cup self-raising/self-rising flour, sifted

For the decoration

150 g/5 oz. white chocolate

150 g/5 oz. red Candy Melts (see chocolatey tip)

100 g/7 tablespoons butter, softened

½ teaspoon pure vanilla extract

100 g/¾ cup icing/ confectioners' sugar, sifted

pink gel or paste food colouring

30 g/1½ packed cups fresh mint

12- or 24-hole cake pop mould, greased with sunflower oil

disposable piping/pastry bag (optional)

baking sheet lined with baking parchment

24 cake pop sticks

cake pop holder (see cake pop tip)

disposable piping/pastry bag fitted with a small star nozzle/tip

pink ribbon

MAKES 24

Preheat the oven to 180°C (350°F) Gas 4.

With an electric hand whisk, cream the butter and sugar until pale and fluffy, then beat in the egg and vanilla extract. Fold through the flour.

Spoon the batter into the prepared cake-pop mould or fill the disposable piping/pastry bag (if using) with the batter, snip a 2-cm/¾-inch hole in the tip, twist the top, and use to fill the mould. Bake for 10 minutes (if you have a 12-hole cake pop mould you will need to do this in batches). Cool in the mould for 5 minutes, then remove and allow to cool on a wire rack.

Put the white chocolate and Candy Melts each into small heatproof bowls set over pans of gently simmering water to melt (see chocolatey tip).

Take 12 cake pop sticks and dip each about 1 cm/⅜ inch into the white melted chocolate, then insert each one into a cake ball and put onto the prepared baking sheet. Take the remaining 12 cake pop sticks and dip into the red Candy Melts and complete in the same way. Freeze for 20 minutes, until the stick is securely fixed to the cake ball. Leave the bowls of chocolate over the hot pans of water (but off the heat).

After 20 minutes, return the pans to the heat and re-melt the remaining chocolate and Candy Melts. Take each cake pop and swirl quickly in either the chocolate or Candy Melts, then put into the cake pop holder to keep upright whilst setting. Put in the fridge for 30 minutes to set completely.

Meanwhile, make the buttercream. Beat the butter and vanilla extract until smooth and pale, then gradually add the icing/confectioners' sugar and beat until smooth and creamy. Colour it a pale to mid-pink shade with the food colouring. Fill the disposable piping/pastry bag fitted with a small star nozzle/tip with the buttercream and pipe a swirl on top of each cake pop. Tie together in bunches with sprigs of mint using pink ribbon.

Chocolatey tip:
Candy Melts and some brands of white chocolate may need thinning a little. After melting, stir through a little vegetable fat, such as Trex or Cookeen, if necessary. Stir until fully melted.

Cake pop tip:
If you don't have a cake pop holder, always look out for blocks of polystyrene in packaging – it makes the perfect stand for setting cake pops!

SPECTACULAR CELEBRATIONS

Bonfire night bonanza

A sparkler of a cake that is perfect for customising. You can also try topping with pieces of tiffin, honeycomb or even toffee apples!

1 quantity of Double Chocolate Sponge mixture (see page 16) baked in three greased and lined 18-cm/7-inch cake pans for 40 minutes until an inserted cocktail stick/toothpick comes out clean, then cooled

1 quantity of Classic Buttercream (see page 20)

purple and blue gel or paste food colouring

175 g/6 oz. chocolate-coated biscuit/cookie fingers, such as Cadbury Fingers

40 g/1 cup mini marshmallows

1 teaspoon small gold sugar balls, to decorate

1 tablespoon large gold sugar balls, to decorate

4 chocolate sticks, such as Matchmakers, broken into pieces

25 g/1 oz. chocolate-coated malt balls, such as Maltesers or Whoppers

edible gold spray

For the fireworks

100 g/3¹/₂ oz. each green, red, orange and yellow clear hard-boiled sweets/hard candies

3 large baking sheets lined with baking parchment

5 wooden skewers

cook's blowtorch (optional)

SERVES 22

If necessary, trim the tops of the cakes to make level. Sandwich together using 350 g/12 oz. of the buttercream – the bottom side of the top cake should be facing up. Place the cake on a serving plate or cake board.

Stir enough purple and blue colouring through the remaining buttercream to get a deep 'night sky' colour. Crumb-coat (see page 11) the cake using 450 g/1 lb. of the buttercream. Place in the fridge to chill for 15 minutes, then use the remaining buttercream to coat the cake in a second layer. Smooth and remove the excess buttercream with a palette knife/metal spatula.

For the fireworks, in a mini food processor, process each of the different colour hard-boiled sweets/hard candies separately to a sugar-like consistency.

Put the green 'sugar' in a very small saucepan and gently heat until melted. Shake the pan towards the end to allow any unmelted 'sugar' to melt. Spoon a small amount of melted green sugar onto one of the lined baking sheets and press the blunt end of a skewer into it to create a base. Drizzle some of the melted sugar back and forth over the base to create a firework pattern. Repeat with the remaining skewers and baking sheets, and allow to set.

Repeat with the red, orange and yellow 'sugar', drizzling each one over the green bases to create five multi-coloured fireworks. You will need only three fireworks for the cake, but it is a good idea to have a couple of spare skewers in case of mistakes.

Using a vegetable peeler, scrape a little chocolate from the biscuit/cookie fingers and break into different lengths. Position around the base of the cake (leaving one-quarter clear for the marshmallows), pressing them gently into the buttercream to create a sky-line effect. Fill the gap with mini marshmallows working up to a point towards the top of the cake. Use a cook's blowtorch to scorch the marshmallows, if liked, to get a 'toasted' effect. Gently press the small and large gold sugar balls into the top and sides of the cake.

Place the Matchmakers around the top edge of the cake. Spray the chocolate balls with gold spray and place on top of the cake. Insert three 'fireworks' into the top. Spray the sides of the cake with little 'bursts' of gold spray, if liked.

Decorating tip:
You can make and ice the cakes up to two days in advance, but it is best to make the fireworks on the day of serving.

Fallen fruit chocolate cake

Try this beautiful sophisticated cake with my luxurious vegan chocolate sponge and brilliant white buttercream for a dairy-free ode to all things autumn/fall!

1 quantity of Vegan Chocolate Sponge mixture (see page 19) baked in three greased and lined 18-cm/7-inch cake pans for 30–35 minutes until an inserted cocktail stick/toothpick comes out clean, then cooled OR 1 quantity of Double Chocolate Sponge mixture (see page 16) baked in three greased and lined 18-cm/7-inch cake pans for 40 minutes until an inserted cocktail stick/toothpick comes out clean, then cooled

$^1/_2$ quantity of Classic Buttercream (see page 20) or Brilliant White Buttercream (see page 21)

3–5 walnut halves

few blackberries, to decorate

edible gold spray

4 sheets of edible gold leaf (optional)

2 figs, one halved, one quartered

3–5 physalis

For the apple and pear crisps

3 Gala apples

3 pears

orange, red, purple and green gel or paste food colouring

2–3 large baking sheets lined with baking parchment

paintbrush

2 wooden skewers

SERVES 22

For the apple and pear crisps, preheat the oven to 80°C (160°F) Gas $^1/_4$. Slice the apples widthways and the pears lengthways with a mandoline to get thin slices (or use a sharp knife and aim to get the slices as thin as possible). Flick out any seeds, then arrange the slices on the prepared baking sheets. Bake for 1$^1/_2$ hours or until dried out.

Fill four small bowls with about 1 cm/$^3/_8$ inch of water. Add a little of each of the food colourings to each of the bowls to get the four different colours. Use the paintbrush to brush the dried apple and pear slices with the colours, as liked – make sure you clean the brush every time you change colour.

Return the coloured fruit to the oven for a further 30 minutes to dry. Remove from the oven and leave to cool on a wire rack (see storage tip).

If necessary, trim the tops of the cakes to make level. Sandwich the cakes together using 300 g/10$^1/_2$ oz. of the buttercream – the bottom side of the top cake should be facing up. Place the cake on a serving plate or cake board. Crumb-coat (see page 11) the cake using the remaining icing. This will be your final coating giving it a semi-naked look, so be sure to scrape off enough icing to reveal some of the sponge.

Spray the walnut halves and some of the blackberries with the gold spray, then decorate using some of the edible gold leaf (if using). Set aside to dry.

Break the skewers into different heights and insert into the top of the cake with the points facing up. Push some of the figs and/or the physalis onto the skewers so that they stand upright and are piled one on top of another.

Position the fruit crisps to the side and on top of the cake, as liked.

Add the blackberries and walnuts to the cake, along with any remaining figs and physalis, as liked. Decorate parts of the figs with the remaining sheet of gold leaf (if using). Spray the whole cake with a fine mist of edible gold spray.

Storage tip:

You may have a few extra crisps left over – these will keep in an airtight container for up to 1 week. Enjoy as a snack.

Fright night cake

1 quantity of Double Chocolate Sponge mixture (see page 16) baked in three greased and lined 18-cm/7-inch cake pans for 40 minutes until an inserted cocktail stick/toothpick comes out clean, then cooled

1 quantity of Classic Buttercream (see page 20)

black gel or paste food colouring

100 g/3½ oz. seedless raspberry jam/jelly

For the cookies

100 g/7 tablespoons butter

100 g/½ cup soft brown sugar

1 egg, beaten

few drops of pure vanilla extract

275 g/2 cups plain/all-purpose flour, sifted, plus extra for dusting

200 g/7 oz. black fondant icing

150 g/5 oz. orange fondant icing

150 g/5 oz. white fondant icing

black and green writing icing pens

1 teaspoon each chocolate flake sprinkles and chocolate pearls

For the fruit syrup

375 g/13 oz. frozen mixed summer fruits

4 tablespoons caster/superfine sugar

2 teaspoons arrowroot powder mixed with 2 teaspoons water

1 set of Halloween cutters

6–8 wooden skewers

2 baking sheets lined with baking parchment

1 disposable piping/pastry bag

small round nozzle/tip

small-medium round nozzle/tip

SERVES 28

For the cookies, cream the butter and brown sugar together, then stir through the egg and vanilla extract. Stir through the flour. Turn out onto a lightly floured work surface and press together to form a ball of dough. Wrap in clingfilm/plastic wrap and place in the freezer for 30 minutes to chill.

Roll the dough out to 4 mm/⅛–¼ inch thick. Using the Halloween cutters, stamp out 16–18 shapes (you will not need them all for the cake). Insert skewers into 6–8 of the cookies. Cut out small rectangles from the trimmings for gravestones. Place on the lined baking sheets. Chill for 30 minutes. Meanwhile, preheat the oven to 180°C (350°F) Gas 4. Bake the cookies for 10–12 minutes until just golden. Cool on a wire rack.

Roll out the fondant icings 2–3 mm/1/16–⅛ inch thick on a work surface lightly dusted with icing/confectioners' sugar. Use the Halloween cutters to stamp out shapes to fit the cookies and stick on with a little water (reserve the black trimmings). Score lines down the pumpkins with the blunt side of a dinner knife. Use the black icing pen to write RIP or spooky dates onto the gravestones.

Use the green icing pen to pipe detail onto the cookies. Attach the chocolate flake sprinkles to the wet green icing for the cat's eyes. Use the reserved black fondant to decorate the pumpkins, sticking the shapes on with water. Use the small-medium round piping nozzle/tip to cut out mouths of the ghosts and use the black icing pen to attach the chocolate pearl sprinkles for eyes.

Trim the tops of the cakes to make level, if necessary. Remove 75 g/2½ oz. of the buttercream and colour it grey. Set aside. Sandwich together using 350 g/12 oz. of the remaining buttercream and the jam/jelly – the bottom side of the top cake should be facing up. Place on a cake board. Crumb-coat (see page 11) the cake using 450 g/1 lb. of the buttercream. Place in the fridge for 15 minutes, then use the remaining buttercream to coat the cake in a second layer. Smooth and remove the excess buttercream with a palette knife/metal spatula. Smear on small blobs of the reserved grey buttercream, then smooth and remove the excess.

For the fruit syrup, heat the fruits in a pan with the caster/superfine sugar and 3 tablespoons of cold water for 10 minutes, until the fruits are broken down. Strain into another pan. Return to the heat for 2–3 minutes until thickened, then stir through the arrowroot mixture and gradually stir through 3½ tablespoons of just-boiled water. Heat until thickened and glossy. Leave to cool, stirring occasionally. Drizzle the syrup over the cake (stir in a little water if it has thickened too much) and add the cookies at different heights.

Christmas shimmer baubles

Not just for the tree – these cakey Christmas shimmer baubles are perfect for offering to guests over the festive period and go down rather well with a little drop of sherry...

½ quantity of Traditional Vanilla Sponge mixture (see page 14) baked in 12 cupcake cases in a muffin pan for 25 minutes, then cooled

100 g/7 tablespoons butter, softened

200 g/scant 1½ cups icing/confectioners' sugar, sifted, plus extra for dusting

150 g/5 oz. green fondant icing

150 g/5 oz. pink fondant icing

175 g/6 oz. silver fondant icing

½ quantity of Royal Icing (see page 22)

2 teaspoons edible glitter

8-cm/3¼-inch round pastry/cookie cutter

cocktail stick/toothpick

disposable piping/pastry bag fitted with a small round nozzle/tip

decorative string/twine (optional)

MAKES 12

Trim any cracks in the tops of the cakes to make smooth dome shapes, if necessary. To buttercream the tops, beat the butter until pale and creamy, then beat in the icing/confectioners' sugar with 2 teaspoons of water until smooth and creamy.

Spread the buttercream on the tops of the cakes with a dinner knife as smoothly as possible. Freeze for 20 minutes, then use your fingers to smooth down any bumps.

Roll out each of the coloured fondant icings, on a work surface lightly dusted with icing/confectioners' sugar, to approximately 3 mm/⅛ inch thick. Using the round cutter, stamp out four 8-cm/3¼-inch rounds from each colour, re-rolling the trimmings as necessary. Use to cover the buttercream base.

For the hanging detail, work on one at a time; for the base section, roll a pea-sized ball using a piece of the silver fondant trimmings, pierce with a cocktail stick/toothpick and thread onto it so the stick goes all the way through, then gently press the sides to flatten slightly whilst widening the hole slightly, and then remove and make indentations around the outside with the side of the cocktail stick/toothpick. Roll a thin sausage shape from some of the remaining silver fondant trimmings, make a loop in the middle, press the ends together and insert into the hole of the base. Set aside and repeat until you have 12 'silver hangers'.

Fill the piping/pastry bag fitted with a small round nozzle/tip with the royal icing. Use to stick the 'silver hangers' to the cakes. Place in different positions on each cake for a really effective look. Pipe Christmas bauble-style designs onto the cakes, go as simple or elaborate as you like. From dots to swirls to a snow scene – anything goes! Bear in mind the rounded shape of the bauble and where the 'silver hanger' is when piping your design for a real 3D feel. Thread and tie some decorative string/twine through the 'hangers', if you like. Sprinkle with plenty of edible glitter.

Wild birch Christmas cake

A plastic robin or reindeer takes me back to digging excitedly through my mum's baking drawer to decorate our traditional Christmas cake. Here they get a modern makeover!

1 quantity of Double Chocolate Sponge mixture (see page 16) baked in three greased and lined 18-cm/7-inch cake pans for 40 minutes until an inserted cocktail stick/ toothpick comes out clean, then cooled

1 quantity of Classic Buttercream (see page 20)

40 g/generous ½ cup desiccated/dry unsweetened shredded coconut

For the wild birch bark

50 g/2 oz. dark/bittersweet chocolate, chopped

300 g/10½ oz. white chocolate

2 baking sheets lined with baking parchment

thin paintbrush

retro Christmas cake decorations

SERVES 22

For the wild birch bark, melt the dark/bittersweet chocolate in a heatproof bowl set over a pan of simmering water (or microwave on high in 30-second bursts, stirring in between). Place the lined baking sheets so they are in a 'landscape' position in front of you. Using the paintbrush dipped in the dark/ bittersweet chocolate, brush small horizontal lines and 'knots' on the baking sheet (see chocolatey tip). Place the sheets in the fridge for 5 minutes to set.

Meanwhile, melt the white chocolate in a separate heatproof bowl set over a pan of simmering water (or microwave on high in 30-second bursts, stirring in between). Remove the baking sheets from the fridge. Working on one sheet at a time, spoon over the white chocolate and spread out to a thin layer using a palette knife/metal spatula. Return to the fridge for 15 minutes.

With the shortest side of the baking sheet facing you, gently roll up the baking parchment, allowing the bark to snap into thin-rectangular pieces. It doesn't matter if you have a few irregular shards, these will still look really effective. Chill until needed.

If necessary, trim the tops of the cakes to make level. Sandwich together using 350 g/12 oz. of the buttercream – the bottom side of the top cake should be facing up. Place the cake on a serving plate or cake board.

Crumb-coat (see page 11) the cake using 450 g/1 lb. of the buttercream. Place in the fridge to chill for 15 minutes, then use the remaining buttercream to coat the cake in a second layer. Smooth and remove the excess buttercream with a palette knife/metal spatula – you don't need to be too neat here as the whole cake will be covered in decoration.

Gently press the bark into the sides of the cake, working around, until the sides are covered. Sprinkle over the desiccated/dried unsweetened shredded coconut, then position the Christmas cake decorations in place.

Chocolatey tip:

Have a small bowl of warm water nearby. If the chocolate starts to set on the paintbrush, clean the brush off in the warm water. Wipe with a paper towel and continue.

Ice queen frozen cake

1 quantity of Traditional Vanilla Sponge mixture baked in three greased and lined 18-cm/7-inch cake pans for 35–40 minutes until an inserted cocktail stick/toothpick comes out clean, then cooled

1 quantity of Brilliant White Buttercream (see page 21)

blue gel or paste food colouring

½ quantity of Royal Icing (see page 22)

large readymade edible snowflakes (optional)

For the chocolate decorations

160 g/5¾ oz. white chocolate or 'bright white' Candy Melts

50 g/2 oz. blue Candy Melts

1 tablespoon miniature meringue sprinkles

1 teaspoon white sugar pearls

½ teaspoon blue sprinkles

For the candy decorations

195 g/7 oz. hard-boiled mints/ hard candy mints, such as Fox's Glacier Mints

20 g/¾ oz. blue raspberry pips (optional)

1 teaspoon white sugar pearls

1 teaspoon edible silver star confetti

1 teaspoon edible silver glitter

piping/pastry bag fitted with a small round nozzle/tip

3 simple snowflake templates

baking sheet lined with baking parchment

cocktail stick/toothpick

baking sheet, lightly greased

1–3 silicone snow flake moulds, 5 cm/2 inches wide and 1 cm/³⁄₈ inch deep (optional)

SERVES 20

For the chocolate snowflakes, melt the white chocolate or Candy Melts in a heatproof bowl set over a pan of simmering water (or microwave on high in 30-second bursts, stirring in between). Fill the piping/pastry bag fitted with a small round nozzle/tip. Place a snowflake template on a baking sheet and cover with a sheet of baking parchment. Use as a guide to pipe snowflakes. Transfer to the freezer until needed. Squeeze any remaining chocolate back into the bowl set over the hot water (off the heat) to keep warm.

For the chocolate white and blue ice shards, melt the blue Candy Melts as above. Pour the remaining melted white chocolate over the lined baking sheet, then drizzle over the melted blue Candy Melts and swirl with a cocktail stick/toothpick. Just before it sets completely, scatter with miniature meringue sprinkles, white sugar pearls and blue sprinkles. Chill to set completely. Break into shards. Chill until needed.

For the clear ice shards, whizz the mints in a mini food processor until they resemble granulated sugar (reserve 30 g/1 oz. if you are making the ice snowflakes). Place in a small pan set over a low heat. As it starts to bubble around the edges, shake it gently. Remove from the heat if it gets too hot, then return to the heat and repeat, shaking occasionally, until completely melted. Pour onto the lightly greased baking sheet and spread with a palette knife/metal spatula. Scatter with the white sugar pearls, silver star confetti and silver glitter. Leave to set, then break into shards and set aside.

For the ice snowflakes (if making), whizz the raspberry pips in a mini processor until they resemble granulated sugar. Preheat the oven to 180°C (350°F) Gas 4. Use the reserved mint 'sugar' and raspberry pip 'sugar' to half-fill silicone snowflake mould(s) and then bake for 5–7 minutes until melted. Allow to set, then release from the mould(s). Set aside.

If necessary, trim the tops of the cakes to make level. Colour 150 g/5 oz. of the buttercream blue and set aside. Sandwich the cakes together using 300 g/10½ oz. of the white buttercream – the bottom side of the top cake should be facing up. Place on a serving plate. Crumb-coat (see page 11) the cake using 450 g/ 1 lb. of the buttercream. Chill for 15 minutes, then use the remaining buttercream to coat the cake in a second layer. Smooth with a palette knife/metal spatula. Smear small blobs of the blue buttercream around the cake, then smooth again.

Add a few drops of water to the royal icing, if needed, to make a pouring consistency, then pour the royal icing over the cake, allowing it to drip down the sides. Level the surface. Insert the ice shards, chocolate snowflakes and readymade snowflakes, if using, into the top and add a snowflake to the side.

Easter egg cake

It's the time to treat yourself, so why not go all way with an Easter cake!
Easter eggs on cake – what's not to love?!

1 quantity of Double Chocolate Sponge mixture (see page 16) baked in two greased and lined 20-cm/8-inch cake pans for 50–55 minutes until an inserted cocktail stick/ toothpick comes out clean, then cooled

75 g/2½ oz. white chocolate

yellow gel or paste food colouring

1 large hollow Easter egg, halved

1 medium hollow Easter egg

2 small hollow Easter eggs, halved and/or partially broken

200 g/7 oz. white fondant icing, cubed

90 g/3¼ oz. mini eggs

For the ganache

400 g/14 oz. dark/bittersweet chocolate, 70% minimum cocoa solids, finely chopped

1 tablespoon liquid glucose

400 ml/scant 1¾ cups whipping cream

For the decorative nests

25 g/1 oz. dark/bittersweet chocolate, broken into pieces

25 g/1 oz. rice vermicelli

baking sheet lined with baking parchment

SERVES 30

For the ganache, put the chocolate into a heatproof bowl with the liquid glucose. Heat the cream in a saucepan until just at simmering point (do not allow to boil). Pour over the chocolate whilst stirring with a metal spoon until smooth. Set aside at room temperature and allow to cool, uncovered, for 2–3 hours until the ganache reaches a spreadable consistency (stir well after the first hour).

Meanwhile, make the decorative nests, melt the chocolate in a heatproof bowl set over a pan of simmering water (or microwave on high in 30-second bursts, stirring in between). Stir through the vermicelli until coated. Put clumps of the mixture onto the lined baking sheet to set.

To make two white chocolate 'runny' eggs, cut out two approximate 15-cm/6-inch squares of baking parchment. Melt the white chocolate in a heatproof bowl set over a pan of simmering water (or microwave on high in 30-second bursts, stirring in between). Remove 1 tablespoon for the yolk and stir enough yellow colouring through to get a 'yolk' yellow shade. Using a teaspoon, spoon the melted white chocolate onto the pieces of baking parchment and tease out to make fried egg shapes. Set aside for a few minutes, then add a dollop of the yellow chocolate on top. Before they set completely, to create the 'bend', gently hang from a shelf in the fridge – cans of beans and soup are great weights for holding them in place!

If necessary, trim the tops of the cakes to make level. Sandwich together using 200 g/7 oz. of the thickened ganache – the bottom side of the top cake should be facing up. Place the cake on a serving plate. Use the remaining ganache to coat the top and sides thickly. Once coated, use the tip of a dinner knife to make horizontal textural indentations in the sides.

Use the Easter eggs to decorate the top of the cake.

Beat the fondant icing in a free-standing mixer with a paddle attachment, or whisk in a bowl using an electric hand whisk fitted with the dough hooks, until softened, then gradually add 3–5 tablespoons of water until it becomes a thick but liquid consistency. Remove 1–2 tablespoons of the mixture and stir enough yellow colouring through to get a 'yolk' yellow shade. Use both to drizzle into some of the chocolate egg shells to make 'eggs'. Decorate the remainder of the cake with the mini eggs and decorative nests. Hang one of the 'runny' white chocolate eggs at the front of the cake and one at the back.

Boy or girl baby shower cake

Boy, girl or a surprise? This is a lovely alternative gift if you're going to a baby shower; use pink and blue buttercream for those awaiting a surprise or adjust the colours slightly for those in the know!

1 quantity of Traditional Vanilla Sponge mixture (see page 14) baked in three greased and lined 18-cm/7-inch cake pans for 35–40 minutes until an inserted cocktail stick/toothpick comes out clean, then cooled

1 quantity of Classic Buttercream (see page 20)

250 g/9 oz. blue and pink Smarties or M&M's

small handful of blue and pink bonbons

pink and blue gel or paste food colouring

75 g/3 oz. white flower modelling paste

100 g/³/₄ cup icing/confectioners' sugar

6 Oreo cookies

1 teaspoon pink cake sprinkles

1 teaspoon blue cake sprinkles

400-g/14-oz. empty clean soup can

1 small flower plunger cutter

1 small round nozzle/tip

1 medium round nozzle/tip

thin pink and blue ribbon

6 cocktail sticks/toothpicks

SERVES 24

Trim the tops of the cakes to make level, if necessary. Push the clean soup can into the centre of each cake, twist the can and lift to remove a centre circle of cake. Slice one of the removed pieces in half horizontally and reserve.

Sandwich the cakes together using 300 g/10½ oz. of the buttercream – the bottom side of the top cake should be facing up. Place the cake on a cake plate. Fill the middle with the Smarties or M&M's and blue and pink bonbons, then place the small reserved sponge circle on top to enclose them. Crumb-coat (see page 11) the cake using 450 g/1 lb. of the buttercream.

Colour 225 g/8 oz. of the remaining buttercream pastel pink, leave 225 g/8 oz. white and colour the remaining 300 g/10½ oz. pastel blue.

Using a dinner knife, starting from the bottom, spread the pink buttercream around the sides of the cake so that it comes to about one-third of the way up (see buttercreamy tip). Add the white buttercream above it so two-thirds of the sides are coated in buttercream. Then add the blue buttercream so the sides and top are fully coated. With the tip of the knife, gently blend the buttercreams. Smooth and remove the excess buttercream with a palette knife/metal spatula.

Roll out the flower modelling paste to a 16-cm/6¹/₄-inch square. Use the flower plunger cutter and round nozzles/tips to stamp out rounds and shapes from the square to create a blanket-style pattern. Loosely lay on the top of the cake. Tie the ribbon in bows around the cocktail sticks/toothpicks.

Divide the icing/confectioners' sugar between two bowls, stir 2¹/₂ teaspoons of water through each to get a thick, spreadable consistency (it needs to be thicker than you may think or you may find it will be too runny), add a little more icing/confectioners' sugar or a few drops of water, if necessary. Use the pink and blue colouring to colour each bowl in pastel shades.

Choose a coloured icing to spread onto the top half of a cookie. Scatter with the corresponding colour cake sprinkles. Carefully insert a cocktail stick/toothpick into the cream filling of the cookie, then insert into the cake to decorate and dry. Repeat with the remaining cookies.

Buttercreamy tip:
Try not to overload your knife – it's easier to add small amounts of buttercream often rather than try to sweep large amounts around the sides of the cake.

Triple chocolate drip cake

There'll be chocolatey waves of appreciation with this little number.

1 quantity of Double Chocolate Sponge mixture (see page 16) baked in three greased and lined 18-cm/7-inch cake pans for 40 minutes until an inserted cocktail stick/toothpick comes out clean, then cooled

½ quantity of Two-ingredient Buttercream (see page 20, adding 2 tablespoons unsweetened cocoa powder with the icing/confectioners' sugar)

375 g/13 oz. dark/bittersweet chocolate, 70% minimum cocoa solids, finely chopped

edible gold spray

1 tablespoon liquid glucose

300 ml/1¼ cups whipping cream

200 g/7 oz. milk chocolate, broken into pieces

75 g/2½ oz. white chocolate, broken into pieces

180 g/6¼ oz. milk chocolates

baking sheet lined with baking parchment

wooden skewer

SERVES 26

Trim the tops of the cakes to make level, if necessary. Sandwich together using 325 g/11½ oz. of the buttercream – the bottom side of the top cake should be facing up. Place the cake on an 18-cm/7-inch cake board or the base of an 18-cm/7-inch loose-bottomed cake pan.

Crumb-coat (see page 11) the cake using 425 g/15 oz. of the buttercream. Place in the freezer to firm up for 45 minutes.

To make the chocolate wave, melt 75 g/2½ oz. of the dark/bittersweet chocolate in a heatproof bowl set over a pan of simmering water (or microwave on high in 30-second bursts, stirring in between). Spoon the chocolate onto the lined baking sheet and smear with a knife to a rough 12 x 24-cm/4¾ x 9½-inch rectangle. Wiggle the paper to level the surface. Whilst still wet, cut the paper and chocolate on one side to create one straight-sided edge. Slide a rolling pin and wooden spoon handle under the paper to create a 'wave' pattern. Chill to set. Decorate with the edible gold spray.

When ready to decorate, place the cake (on its 18-cm/7-inch board) on a small upturned sturdy flat-based bowl over a baking sheet lined with clingfilm/plastic wrap. Place the remaining dark/bittersweet chocolate and the liquid glucose in a heatproof bowl. Heat the cream until just at simmering point (do not allow to boil). Pour over the chocolate and glucose and whisk until smooth. Pour around the top edge of the cake allowing it to trickle down the sides, then pour over the top of the cake. Use a palette knife/metal spatula to smooth the top and spread the ganache to cover the sides completely. Transfer to a serving cake plate or new board and smooth the sides with a cake smoother, palette knife/metal spatula. Chill for 1 hour.

Melt the milk chocolate as above. At the same time, melt the white chocolate separately. Remove the cake from the fridge. Pour the melted milk chocolate around the top of the cake, next to the edge, allowing it to trickle down the sides. Continue drizzling the chocolate in a spiral motion moving inwards to completely cover the top of the cake. Gently sweep a long palette knife/metal spatula across the top to smooth the chocolate, if necessary (keep any remaining melted milk chocolate in the bowl over the pan of hot water).

Drop teaspoonfuls of the white chocolate over the milk chocolate and use the skewer to drag swirling patterns through the chocolate. Just before the chocolate sets, position the chocolate wave and first layer of milk chocolates on top of the cake. Build up the chocolates using the remaining melted milk chocolate to secure them in place, allowing it to set for 10–15 minutes between layers, if necessary.

Piñata cake

The ultimate surprise-inside cake, using a petal nozzle/tip here helps to create that carnival-style textured paper look with ease.

1 quantity of Traditional Vanilla Sponge mixture (see page 14) baked in two greased and lined 20-cm/8-inch cake pans for 45–50 minutes until an inserted cocktail stick/toothpick comes out clean, then cooled

1.8 kg/4 lb. Classic Buttercream (see page 20 using quantities: 350 g/3 sticks unsalted butter, 250 g/1¼ cups vegetable fat and 1.2 kg/8½ cups icing/confectioners' sugar)

300 g/10½ oz. small sweets/candies of your choice

yellow, purple, orange, blue, green and red gel or paste food colouring

400-g/14-oz. empty clean soup can

6 small disposable piping/pastry bags

125 Wilton petal nozzle/tip

3 large disposable piping/pastry bags

1 gold glitter piñata donkey (optional – see crafty tip)

SERVES 20

Trim the tops of the cakes, if necessary, to create a flat surface. Push the clean soup can into the centre of each cake, twist the can and lift to remove a centre circle of cake. Slice one of the removed pieces in half horizontally and reserve.

Using 250 g/9 oz. of the buttercream, sandwich the two cakes together. Place the cake on a cake board. Fill the middle with the surprise sweets/candies, then place the small reserved sponge circle on top to enclose them. Place 500 g/1 lb. 2 oz. of the buttercream into a bowl, add enough yellow colouring to get a bright colour. Use to coat the cake with a thick crumb coat (see page 11).

Divide the remaining buttercream between six bowls. Add the purple colouring to the first bowl, the orange to the second, the blue to the third, the yellow to the fourth, the green to the fifth and the red to the sixth. You need to add enough colouring so the colours are bright.

Fill the six small piping/pastry bags each with a different coloured buttercream and snip a 1-cm/⅜-inch hole in the end of each.

Place the petal nozzle/tip inside a large piping/pastry bag. Take two small piping/pastry bags with colours of your choice and insert into the large bag with the petal nozzle/tip, then twist the top.

Carefully pipe around the cake from the bottom; gently squeeze the buttercreams from the piping/pastry bag holding the tip next to the cake with the rounded end at the top and the point at the bottom. Move the nozzle/tip up and down as you work around the cake to get a ruffled effect. Once you have gone around the cake at least once with the first colours, you can start piping the top, working from the outside-in, using the same up-and-down motion but changing to a shallower angle. Carry on until the bag is empty, then wash and dry the nozzle/tip, and repeat twice with a new large piping/pastry bag and two more smaller bags of coloured buttercreams each time.

Once the cake is covered, insert the gold glitter piñata donkey, if using.

Crafty tip:
To make a gold glitter piñata donkey, stick two pieces of gold glittery paper back-to-back. Draw a simple silhouette of a piñata donkey (or print one out) and cut out. Before the glue is fully stuck, gently push a wooden skewer between the two halves. Press to reseal and insert into the cake.

CANDY LAND

Candy shop show-stopper

I'm a sucker for the types of sweets on this cake, they remind me of carefree days and chatty, slow walks home from school with my friend Nic – after saving half our dinner money for the corner shop. Pass me a giant strawberry or foam banana!

1 quantity of Traditional Vanilla Sponge mixture (see page 14)

1 quantity of Classic Buttercream (see page 20)

2 tablespoons colourful cake sprinkles

500 g/1 lb. 2 oz. mixed sweets/candies such as jellies, foam bananas, strawberry laces, flying saucers, jazzies, sugar-coated chocolate beans

muffin case

muffin pan

3 18-cm/7-inch cake pans, greased and lined

wooden skewer

craft glue gun

plastic sweetie/candy jar

cocktail stick/toothpick

SERVES 20

Preheat the oven to 180°C (350°F) Gas 4.

Remove 75 g/2½ oz. of the cake mixture and use to fill the muffin case in the muffin pan. Cover with clingfilm/plastic wrap and set aside. Divide the remaining cake mixture between the three cake pans. Bake the large cakes for 35–40 minutes until an inserted cocktail stick/toothpick comes out clean. Allow the cakes to cool in the pans for 10 minutes, then remove and place on a wire rack to cool completely. Whilst the large cakes are cooling, uncover the muffin in the pan and bake for 25 minutes. Allow to cool.

If necessary, trim the tops of the large cakes to make level. Sandwich together using 350 g/12 oz. of the buttercream – the bottom side of the top cake should be facing up. Place the cake on a serving plate or cake board.

Crumb-coat (see page 11) the cake using 450 g/1 lb. of the buttercream. Remove the muffin from the paper case, trim the rounded top so it is flat and place top-side down to one side on the top of the cake so that it sticks onto the buttercream. Place in the fridge to chill for 15 minutes, then use the remaining buttercream to coat the main cake in a second layer and the muffin in a thick single layer. Smooth and remove the excess buttercream on the main cake with a palette knife/metal spatula.

Place the cake on its serving plate or cake board on a wire rack over a baking sheet. Press the cake sprinkles around the base of the cake. Re-gather any dropped sprinkles and press on again, if necessary.

Press some of the sweets/candies onto the muffin so it is completely hidden. Stick more sweets on the top and to the sides of the cake to give a 'tumbling-feel'. Scatter a few on the cake plate or board, if liked.

The sweets/candies on the skewer are for decoration only. Take the wooden skewer and use a glue gun to stick sweets/candies to the top third, bulk them out so they are 3–4 sweets/candies deep at the base (this will then act as a stopper and hold up the plastic jar). Insert the bare section of the skewer into the muffin and cake, then place the plastic jar over the sweets/candies.

Insert the cocktail stick/toothpick into the top of the cake at the edge and hang the jar lid from it. Gently press the lid into the buttercream for extra support. Remove and discard the skewer and cocktail stick/toothpick when cutting and serving.

Giant jaffa cake

'Go on then, I'll just have one...' This giant Jaffa cake
is especially for those who just can't resist.

For the jelly

135-g pack of UK orange
   jelly/1¼ 3-oz packs of US
   powdered orange jello
100 g/3½ oz. shredless
   marmalade

For the cake

½ quantity of Dessert-style
   Sponge mixture (see page 18)
   baked in a 25-cm/10-inch
   cake pan for 12 minutes,
   then cooled
250 g/9 oz. dark/bittersweet
   chocolate, 70% minimum
   cocoa solids, broken into
   pieces
18-cm/7-inch cake pan,
   greased and lined with
   clingfilm/plastic wrap
wooden skewer

SERVES 10–12

For the jelly, place the jelly cubes/powdered jello into a heatproof jug/
pitcher with the marmalade.

Pour over 350 ml/scant 1½ cups boiling water and stir until dissolved
(if it needs a helping hand to dissolve, place in the microwave on high in
30-second bursts – do not allow to over heat). Pour into the lined cake pan
pan, allow to cool, then transfer to the fridge to set for at least 4 hours.

For the cake, invert the cake so the flattest side is at the top. Remove the
jelly from the pan using the clingfilm/plastic wrap to help. Place on top of
the cake.

Melt the chocolate in a heatproof bowl set over a pan of simmering water
(or microwave on high in 30-second bursts, stirring in between).

Spoon the chocolate over the cake and spread with a palette knife or
metal spatula so there's an even layer over the top. Gently drag criss-cross
patterns in the top using the wooden skewer. Chill to set. Dip a knife in hot
water and dry to cut and serve.

Rocky road muffins

50 g/2 oz. mini marshmallows

75 g/2½ oz. dark/bittersweet chocolate, chopped

½ quantity of Double Chocolate Sponge mixture (see page 16)

For the rocky road shards

250 g/9 oz. dark/bittersweet chocolate, broken into pieces

25 g/1 oz. mini marshmallows, plus extra for scattering

2 digestive biscuits/graham crackers, roughly crushed

For the ganache

100 g/3½ oz. dark/bittersweet chocolate, 70% minimum cocoa solids, grated

100 ml/⅓ cup whipping cream

12-hole muffin pan lined with paper cases

20-cm/8-inch square baking pan, greased and lined with baking parchment

MAKES 12

Preheat the oven to 180°C (350°F) Gas 4. Stir the mini marshmallows and the chopped dark/bittersweet chocolate through the batter. Divide between the paper cases and bake for 25 minutes, until an inserted cocktail stick/toothpick comes out clean. Transfer to a wire rack and allow to cool.

For the rocky road shards, melt the chocolate in a heatproof bowl set over a pan of simmering water (or microwave on high in 30-second bursts, stirring in between). Pour the chocolate into the lined square baking pan and spread out to cover the surface, wiggling the pan a little to level the chocolate. Scatter over the marshmallows and crushed digestive biscuits/graham crackers. Chill until set.

For the ganache, put the chocolate into a heatproof bowl. Heat the cream in a small saucepan until just at simmering point – so it is just bubbling slightly at the edges (do not allow to boil). Pour over the chocolate whilst continually stirring with a metal spoon; continue to stir until the mixture is smooth. Set aside at room temperature and allow to cool, uncovered, for around 45–60 minutes until the ganache has thickened enough to hold its shape but still has a little fluidity.

Break the rocky road into shards. Dig out a little of the middle of each muffin with a teaspoon, fill each with about a tablespoonful of ganache, then push in a rocky road shard. Chill until the ganache has set.

Ferrero rocher cake

A slice of luxury. This mix of melted chocolate with a scattering of hazelnuts and a surprise-inside creamy chocolate centre is a gorgeous, if slightly addictive, treat.

100 g/3½ oz. milk chocolate, chopped

100 g/3½ oz. dark/bittersweet chocolate, 85% minimum cocoa solids, chopped

20 g/⅙ cup chopped toasted hazelnuts, plus an extra 1 tablespoon for sprinkling

1 quantity of Double Chocolate Sponge mixture (see page 16) baked in two greased and lined deep 20-cm/8-inch cake pans for 50–55 minutes, until an inserted cocktail stick/toothpick comes out clean, then cooled

150 ml/⅔ cup Nutella

250 ml/1 cup whipping cream

1 kg/2 lb. 4 oz. Classic Buttercream (see page 20, with quantities 200 g/1¾ sticks butter, 125 g/4½ oz. vegetable fat, 650 g/4⅔ cups icing/confectioners' sugar, plus 3 tablespoons unsweetened cocoa powder added with the icing/confectioners' sugar)

7 Ferrero Rocher chocolates

1–2 sheets edible gold leaf (optional)

disposable piping/pastry bag

baking sheet lined with baking parchment

400-g/14-oz. empty clean soup can

SERVES 24

To make the chocolate discs for the top of the cake, melt 25 g/1 oz. of the milk chocolate and 25 g/1 oz. of the dark/bittersweet chocolate together in a heatproof bowl set over a pan of simmering water (or microwave on high in 30-second bursts, stirring in between). Spoon into the piping/pastry bag and cut a small hole in the tip. Use to drizzle 5–7 circles, 3–5 cm/1¼–2 inches in diameter, onto the lined baking sheet. Fill some completely with chocolate and some with a criss-cross pattern. Sprinkle the 'filled' discs with the 1 tablespoon of chopped hazelnuts. Chill until needed.

If necessary, trim the tops of the cakes to make level. Push the soup can into the centre of each cake, twist the can and lift to remove a centre circle of cake. Slice one of the removed pieces in half horizontally and reserve.

To make the hazelnut chocolate filling, stir the Nutella to loosen. Whip the cream until very soft peaks form. Stir the cream through the Nutella, a couple of tablespoons at a time.

Using 200 g/7 oz. of the buttercream, sandwich the two large cakes together. Place the cake on a cake board. Fill the middle with the chocolate filling, then place the small reserved sponge circle on top to enclose the filling.

Crumb-coat (see page 11) the cake using 350 g/12 oz. of the buttercream. Place in the fridge for 15 minutes, then use the remaining buttercream to coat the cake in a second layer. Smooth and remove the excess buttercream with a palette knife/metal spatula. Chill for 15 minutes.

Melt the remaining milk and dark/bittersweet chocolate, together as above. Stir half of the chopped hazelnuts through the chocolate.

Pour the melted hazelnut chocolate around the top of the cake, next to the edge, allowing it to trickle down the sides. Continue drizzling the chocolate in spiral motion, moving inwards to completely cover the top of the cake (leave a couple of tablespoons of melted chocolate in the bottom of the bowl). Gently sweep a long palette knife/metal spatula across the top to level, if necessary. Gently 'throw' the remaining hazelnuts at the melted chocolate; they will immediately stick. Chill for 30 minutes.

Re-melt the reserved two tablespoons of chocolate, if necessary, and use as a glue to help stick the chocolate and hazelnut discs to the top of the cake along with the Ferrero Rocher chocolates. Decorate with the edible gold leaf, if using. Serve at room temperature and use a warmed knife to cut.

Dunkin' doughnuts cake

pink gel or paste food colouring

1 quantity of Royal Icing
(see page 22)

16–20 mini doughnuts

2 teaspoons multi-coloured
sugar strands

turquoise gel or paste food
colouring

1 quantity of Double Chocolate
Sponge mixture (see page 16)
baked in three greased and
lined 18-cm/7-inch cake pans
for 40 minutes until an inserted
cocktail stick/toothpick comes
out clean, then cooled

1 quantity of Classic
Buttercream (see page 20)

4–5 wooden skewers

SERVES 26

This makes a great wow-factor birthday cake. I love using these colour-clashing brights, but anything goes – you can even create it in the birthday girl's or boy's favourite footie team colours!

Add enough pink colouring to the royal icing to get a bright shade of pink.

Place the doughnuts on a wire rack over a baking sheet (to catch any drips). Spread the tops with some of the pink icing. Scatter over the sugar strands. Cover the remaining icing with clingfilm/plastic wrap, and set aside.

If necessary, trim the tops of the cakes to make level. Sandwich together using 350 g/12 oz. of the buttercream – the bottom side of the top cake should be facing up. Place the cake on a serving plate or cake board.

Add enough of the turquoise colouring to the remaining buttercream to get a bright shade. Remember it will darken slightly on standing. Crumb-coat (see page 11) the cake using 450 g/1 lb. of the buttercream. Place in the fridge for 15 minutes, then use the remaining buttercream to coat the cake in a second layer. Smooth and remove the excess buttercream with a palette knife/metal spatula.

Give the pink icing a stir to loosen and add a few drops of water, if necessary to give it a thick but pourable consistency. Spoon the pink icing over the top of the cake, next to the edge, allowing it to trickle down one side.

Break the skewers, so they are different lengths, then insert into the cake so the points are facing up. Use the skewers to position and secure the doughnuts on the cake – it looks particularly effective if a few doughnuts are vertical (without the skewer showing!). Allow to set before serving.

For gluten-free:

Use 1 quantity of Gluten-free Double Chocolate Sponge mixture (see page 17) baked in three 18-cm/7-inch cake pans for 40 minutes, until an inserted cocktail stick/toothpick comes out clean. Allow to cool before using. Use gluten-free mini doughnuts. Always check ingredients on individual products (such as sprinkles) to make sure that the product is gluten-free.

After eight mini cakes

½ quantity of Double Chocolate Sponge mixture (see page 16) baked in a greased and lined deep 20-cm/8-inch square cake pan for 40–45 minutes until an inserted cocktail stick/toothpick comes out clean, then cooled

18 thin square mint-filled chocolates, such as After Eights

For the ganache topping

150 g/5 oz. dark/bittersweet chocolate, 70% minimum cocoa solids, very finely chopped

150 ml/⅔ cup whipping cream

For the mint shards

150 g/5 oz. white chocolate, chopped

green gel or paste food colouring

½ teaspoon chocolate sprinkles

2 hard-boiled mints/hard candy mints, such as Fox's Glacier Mints, crushed with a pestle and mortar

For the buttercream filling

75 g/¾ stick butter, softened

150 g/1 cup icing/confectioners' sugar, sifted

few drops of mint extract

green gel or paste food colouring

6-cm/2½-inch pastry/ cookie cutter

baking sheet lined with baking parchment

disposable piping/pastry bag fitted with a small star nozzle/tip

MAKES 9

For the hostess with the mostest. Allow some space for these lovely little minty numbers – the perfect way to end a dinner party.

Mark out nine 6-cm/2½-inch rounds using the pastry/cookie cutter on the top of the sponge – gently press into the top of the cake. Use a thin sharp knife to follow the marks and cut out small round cakes. Transfer the cakes to the freezer for 20 minutes. Remove from the freezer and cut each twice horizontally to make three layers.

For the ganache topping, put the chocolate into a heatproof bowl. Heat the cream in a small saucepan, until just at simmering point – so it is just bubbling slightly at the edges (do not allow to boil). Pour over the chocolate whilst continually stirring with a metal spoon; continue to stir until the mixture is smooth. Set aside at room temperature and allow to cool, uncovered, for around 45 minutes until the ganache has thickened enough to hold its shape but still has a little fluidity.

Whilst the ganache is cooling, make the mint shards. Melt the white chocolate in a heatproof bowl set over a pan of simmering water (or microwave on high in 30 second bursts, stirring in between). Stir through a little green colouring to get a mint-shade. Spoon over the lined baking sheet and spread out to a 12 x 20-cm/4½ x 8-inch rectangle. Scatter over the chocolate sprinkles and crushed mints. Freeze until needed.

Place the top layer of each cake onto a work surface. Spoon the thickened ganache on the top of each sponge. Set aside for around 15 minutes for the ganache to firm up a little more – it needs to be fairly soft but firm enough to support the weight of the toppings.

Break the mint-coloured chocolate rectangle into shards, gently push a shard into the ganache of each cake top along with two mint-filled chocolates. Set aside whilst you prepare the buttercream filling.

Beat the butter until pale and creamy, then beat in the icing/confectioners' sugar with 2 teaspoons of water until smooth and creamy. Stir through the mint extract and enough green colouring to get a mint-green shade. Fill the piping/pastry bag fitted with a small star nozzle/tip with the buttercream. Sandwich the two remaining layers of each cake together with little stars of buttercream. Pipe another layer of stars on top, then carefully top each with the decorated top layer. Chill until ready to serve.

Red velvet crepe cake

vegetable oil spray

1 tablespoon pink heart-shaped
   sprinkles

For the batter

150 g/generous 1 cup plain/
   all-purpose flour, sifted

3 tablespoons unsweetened
   cocoa powder

pinch of salt

50 g/$\frac{1}{4}$ cup caster/superfine
   sugar

3 eggs, beaten

250 ml/1 cup milk

150 ml/$\frac{2}{3}$ cup soured/sour
   cream

1 tablespoon pure vanilla extract

red gel or paste food colouring

For the cream cheese filling

375 g/$2\frac{2}{3}$ cups icing/
   confectioners' sugar, sifted

750 g/$3\frac{1}{3}$ cups full-fat cream
   cheese

*disposable piping/pastry
   bag fitted with a large
   star nozzle/tip*

SERVES 20

For the pancake batter, mix the dry ingredients together in a bowl, then create a well in the centre. Mix the wet ingredients together in a jug/pitcher (except the food colouring) and gradually pour into the well, gently whisking to mix the wet and dry ingredients together. Stir through enough red food colouring to get a mid-bright shade.

Spray a 17-cm/6$\frac{3}{4}$-inch (measured across the base) frying pan/skillet with the oil spray and heat over a medium heat. Add a small ladleful of the batter to the pan. Tilt the pan so the batter covers the base and then cook for around 30–60 seconds until cooked underneath. Flip or turn the pancake and cook for another 30–60 seconds. Remove, then re-spray the pan with the oil spray and repeat. You should get around 20 pancakes. Allow to cool.

For the filling, beat the icing/confectioners' sugar into the cream cheese, in manageable batches, with an electric hand whisk until smooth. Put 150 g/5 oz. of the mixture into a small bowl, cover and chill whilst you use the remaining filling to stack the pancakes.

Stack the pancakes with a layer of the cream cheese filling between each. Fill the piping/pastry bag fitted with a large star nozzle/tip with the reserved chilled filling and pipe small star-shaped blobs around the top edge. Scatter with the sprinkles. Chill for at least 2 hours before serving.

Dazzling mallow teacake 'cakes'

There's something about that fluffy marshmallow treat that brings joy to all generations. Here's my big cakey version with a little extra va-va-voom.

½ quantity of Dessert-style Sponge mixture (see page 18) baked in a 30 x 22-cm/12 x 8¾-inch baking Swiss roll/jelly roll pan for 20 minutes, then cooled

300 g/10½ oz. dark/bittersweet chocolate, minimum 85% cocoa solids, broken into pieces

1 tablespoon lilac cake sprinkles

edible iridescent lilac lustre

For the marshmallow filling

3 gelatine leaves

3 egg whites

175 g/generous ¾ cup caster/superfine sugar

good pinch of salt

purple gel or paste food colouring

8-cm/3¼-inch pastry/cookie cutter

large disposable piping/pastry bag

baking sheet lined with clingfilm/plastic wrap

MAKES 6

Using the 8-cm/3¼-inch pastry/cookie cutter, stamp out six rounds from the sponge. If it doesn't pierce all the way to the bottom of the sponge, gently push down as far as the cutter will go, then follow the line with a sharp knife to cut out completely. Set aside.

For the marshmallow filling, put the gelatine into a bowl of cold water and set aside to soften. Put the egg whites, caster/superfine sugar, 1 tablespoon of water and the salt into a heatproof bowl. Place over a pan of gently simmering water, whisk with an electric hand whisk until thick and leaving a trail from the beaters – this will take about 5 minutes.

When the marshmallow mixture is thick, remove the bowl from the heat. Working quickly, squeeze the excess water from the gelatine leaves. Add a little of the purple colouring to the marshmallow and continue whisking whilst you add the gelatine leaves one at a time. Whisk for another 3–5 minutes until the marshmallow has cooled slightly and is getting really stiff.

Transfer to the piping/pastry bag and cut a 3-cm/1¼-inch hole in the tip. Pipe a blob of marshmallow onto a sponge base – keep gently squeezing on the bag until the marshmallow spreads and covers the base, then pull away. There may be a pointy tip, so you can dab this down a little with a wetted finger, if liked. Repeat with the remaining bases and marshmallow. Leave to set for 40 minutes.

To coat the teacakes in chocolate, put the teacakes on a wire rack set over the lined baking sheet.

Melt the chocolate in a heatproof bowl set over a pan of simmering water (or microwave on high in 30-second bursts, stirring in between) until very runny.

Spoon the chocolate over the cakes until coated. If necessary, to gather the excess chocolate, give the wire rack a gentle tap and move to stand over another baking sheet. Use the clingfilm/plastic wrap to help gather up the excess dripped chocolate, then return the chocolate to the bowl and use to coat any gaps or the last teacakes.

Before the teacakes have set fully on the wire rack, transfer to a sheet of baking parchment. Scatter with the lilac sprinkles. Once fully set, sprinkle with the edible lustre.

50 g/3½ tablespoons butter, softened

100 g/¾ cup icing/confectioners' sugar, sifted

400 g/14 oz. readymade Madeira cake or ¼ quantity of Traditional Vanilla Sponge mixture (see page 14) baked in a greased and lined 450-g/1-lb loaf pan for 25–30 minutes, then cooled

200 g/7 oz. milk chocolate, broken into pieces

12 ice cream cones (with a sharp knife, use a gentle sawing motion to cut off the flared tops)

1 teaspoon multi-coloured sugar strands

1 teaspoon chopped toasted nuts

1 tablespoon mini fudge pieces

200 g/7 oz. white chocolate, broken into pieces

200 g/7 oz. pink Candy Melts (or white chocolate, broken into pieces – stir in a dab of pink food colouring suitable for chocolate after melting)

baking sheet lined with baking parchment

MAKES 12

Melting ice cream drippy cakes

To make a simple buttercream, beat the butter with an electric hand whisk, add 1 teaspoon of water and gradually add the icing/confectioners' sugar, whisking well between each addition.

Crumble the cake into fine crumbs into a mixing bowl. Stir the buttercream into the crumbs, then use your hands to combine to ensure it's mixed together well and evenly. Shape the mixture into 12 balls.

Melt the milk chocolate in a heatproof bowl set over a pan of simmering water (or microwave on high in 30-second bursts, stirring in between). Working quickly, place one of the balls in the melted milk chocolate and turn to coat, drizzle a teaspoonful of the chocolate onto the lined baking sheet, then using a spoon to help, place the ball on top. Drizzle over a little more melted chocolate, if liked. Leave to set for a few minutes, then place a cone on top and scatter with the decorations of your choice. Repeat with three more of the cake pop balls. Leave to set completely.

Repeat with the white chocolate and then repeat with the pink Candy Melts (see chocolatey tip).

Chocolatey tip:
If using Candy Melts, they may need thinning a little – after melting, stir through a little vegetable fat, if necessary, such as Trex or Cookeen. Stir until fully melted.

Britalian trifle layer cake

Welcome to my Britalian kitchen! A cake with everything I love about the great traditional British trifle combined with a scoop of super-cool Italian flavour.

1 quantity of Dessert-style Sponge mixture (see page 18) baked in two greased and lined deep 20-cm/8-inch cake pans for 25 minutes until an inserted cocktail stick/toothpick comes out clean, then cooled

125 g/generous 1/3 cup seedless raspberry jam/jelly

150 g/generous 1 cup raspberries

150 g/generous 1 cup blackberries

225 g/2 cups strawberries, halved, larger ones quartered

200 g/1 1/2 cups blueberries

300 ml/1 1/4 cups whipping cream

400 g/1 3/4 cups mascarpone

100 g/3/4 cup icing/confectioners' sugar, sifted

3 tablespoons sweet sherry

3 tablespoons custard powder

mint leaves, to decorate

20 g/3/4 oz. dark/bittersweet chocolate, cut into fine shards

For the croccante

200 g/1 cup caster/superfine sugar

50 g/generous 1/3 cup whole blanched (skinned) almonds, toasted (see nutty tip)

50 g/scant 2/3 cup flaked/slivered almonds, toasted (see nutty tip)

baking sheet, greased with sunflower oil

SERVES 16

For the croccante, put the sugar in a saucepan. Cook over a medium heat, without stirring (shake the pan a little, if necessary), until the sugar melts and turns a golden colour. Add the almonds and carry on cooking for 1 minute. Pour onto the oiled baking sheet and leave to cool and set. Roughly break up the croccante into shards. Set aside.

Trim the tops of the cakes to make level, if necessary, then cut each cake in half horizontally.

Stir the jam/jelly to loosen, then gently stir through all the fruit.

Whisk the cream until medium-stiff peaks form. In a separate bowl, whisk the mascarpone with the icing/confectioners' sugar, sweet sherry and custard powder. Fold in the whipped cream.

Sandwich the cakes together using three-quarters of the cream mixture and most of the fruit. Place the final cake layer on top and spread with the remaining cream mixture. Decorate with the remaining fruit, the mint leaves, croccante and chocolate shards.

Nutty tip:

To toast the almonds, preheat the oven to 180°C (350°F) Gas 4. Spread the almonds on a small baking sheet and roast for 5 minutes until they are a light golden colour. Leave to cool.

Sprinkle spectacular cake

1 quantity of Traditional Vanilla Sponge mixture (see page 14) baked in three greased and lined 18-cm/7-inch cake pans for 35–40 minutes until an inserted cocktail stick/toothpick comes out clean, then cooled

1 quantity of Brilliant White Buttercream (see page 21)

240 g/8^1/$_2$ oz. hundreds-and-thousands/multi-coloured sprinkles

50 g/2 oz. white sugar pearls

175 g/6 oz. dark/bittersweet chocolate, 85% cocoa solids, chopped

For the bow

icing/confectioners' sugar, for dusting

40 g/1^1/$_2$ oz. white flower modelling paste

60 g/2^1/$_4$ oz. pink flower modelling paste

60 g/2^1/$_4$ oz. yellow flower modelling paste

60 g/2^1/$_4$ oz. blue flower modelling paste

several wooden spoons

SERVES 20

For the bow, on a work surface dusted with icing/confectioners' sugar, roll out the coloured modelling pastes to as thin as you can get them. Using a combination of colours, cut into 18 strips that are 11 x 1.5-cm/4^1/$_4$ x ^{1}/$_2$ inch and nine strips that are 8 x 1.5 cm/3^1/$_4$ x ^{1}/$_2$ inch. Fold each strip in half and stick the ends together with a little water to create a loop. Cut the stuck-together ends into points so they fit together snugly when positioned on top of the cake. Thread the loops onto wooden spoons to keep their shape.

Roll the trimmings from the pink, yellow and blue modelling pastes into 20 cm/8 inch long sausage shapes. Flatten each one with a rolling pin to as thin as you can get it. Trim each into a strip that is 20 x 1.5 cm/8 x ^{1}/$_2$ inch. Wrap the strips around the handles of wooden spoons in a spiral shape. Set both the loops and spirals aside for at least 3 hours or overnight to harden.

If necessary, trim the tops of the cakes to make level. Reserve 50 g/2 oz. of the buttercream. Sandwich the cakes together using 300 g/10^1/$_2$ oz. of the buttercream – the bottom side of the top cake should be facing up. Place the cake on a serving plate or cake board.

Crumb-coat (see page 11) the cake using 450 g/1 lb. of the buttercream. Place in the fridge for 15 minutes, then use the remaining buttercream to coat the cake in a second layer. Smooth and remove the excess buttercream with a palette knife/metal spatula. Place the cake on its plate or board on a wire rack over a baking sheet. Mix together the hundreds-and-thousands/multi-coloured sprinkles and the sugar pearls. Gently press the sprinkles all over the top and sides of the cake, regathering as necessary, so the cake is completely covered.

Melt the chocolate in a heatproof bowl set over a pan of simmering water (or microwave on high in 30-second bursts, stirring in between). Pour the chocolate around the top of the cake, next to the edge, allowing it to trickle down the sides. Continue drizzling the chocolate in a spiral motion moving inwards to completely cover the top of the cake. Gently sweep a palette knife/metal spatula across the top to smooth the chocolate. Leave to set.

Remove the loops and spirals from the wooden spoons. To build the bow, start with the large loops; use dots of the reserved buttercream to secure in place; start with nine large loops at the base and build up one more layer of nine (trim, if necessary). Then add a layer of small loops. Finish with a single small loop in the centre (trim, if necessary). (If you have any small loops leftover, slot into any gaps, as liked.) Place the spirals at the base of the bow (trim, if necessary), as liked. Use a warmed knife to cut the cake.

PSYCHEDELIC TREATS

Seventies swirl cake

Celebrate any Seventies diva party in style with this
swirly whirly psychedelic cake.

1 quantity of Traditional Vanilla
Sponge mixture (see page 14)

yellow, pink, green, blue, violet
gel or paste food colouring

1 quantity of Classic
Buttercream (see page 20)

1 quantity of Royal Icing
(see page 22)

7–10 large readymade colourful
marshmallow sweets/candies

small handful of colourful
bonbons

2 18-cm/7-inch round cake pans,
greased and lined

cocktail sticks/toothpicks

SERVES 20

Preheat the oven to 180°C (350°F) Gas 4. Divide the sponge batter between five bowls (see cakey tip). Stir a little yellow colouring into one bowl, the pink into one bowl, the green into one bowl, the blue into one bowl, and the violet into the final bowl. Stir in enough colouring so you have mid-bright colours.

Drop spoonfuls of batter into the prepared pans, alternating the colours. Use a cocktail stick/toothpick to swirl the colours gently for a marbled effect. Bake for 35–40 minutes until an inserted cocktail stick/toothpick comes out clean. Allow to cool in the pans for 10 minutes, then remove and place on a wire rack to cool completely.

If necessary, trim the tops of the cakes to make level. Reserve 100 g/3½ oz. of the buttercream – cover and set aside. Sandwich the cakes together using 350 g/12 oz. of the remaining buttercream – the bottom side of the top cake should be facing up. Place the cake on a serving plate or cake board.

Crumb-coat (see page 11) the cake using 450 g/1 lb. of the buttercream. Place in the fridge to chill for 15 minutes, then use the remaining buttercream to coat the cake in a second layer. Smooth and remove the excess buttercream with a palette knife/metal spatula.

You are looking for a fairly runny consistency with the royal icing so that the colours naturally level when they are spooned onto the cake, so add a few drops of water, if necessary. The mixture should coat the back of a spoon and have a good 'flow'. Divide the royal icing between five small bowls and add enough colouring to each to get mid-tone shades.

Drop a spoonful of coloured royal icing on the top of the cake – near the edge, drop a slightly smaller amount in a different colour on top of this, then a third colour, if liked. Use this method to cover the top of the cake, allowing it to naturally trickle down the sides. Use cocktail sticks/toothpicks to swirl the icing a little. Allow to set for at least 4 hours or overnight, then position the marshmallow sweets/candies and bonbons on top – use little blobs of the reserved buttercream to help to secure them in place.

Cakey tip
The total weight of the sponge batter should be around 1.65 kg/3 lb. 10 oz. so each bowl should have around 330 g/11½ oz. of batter.

Mad Hatter's tea party cake

1 quantity of Traditional Vanilla Sponge mixture (see page 14) baked in two deep 20-cm/ 8-inch cake pans for 45–50 minutes until an inserted cocktail stick/toothpick comes out clean, then cooled

1.2 kg/2 lb. 10 oz. Two-ingredient Buttercream (see page 20, with quantities: 400 g/3½ sticks butter and 800 g/5¾ cups icing/confectioners' sugar)

green gel or paste food colouring

2 flat-based ice cream cones

150 g/5 oz. pink fondant icing

edible gold spray (optional)

clear glaze spray (optional)

40 g/1½ oz. each red, green, yellow and blue fondant icing

125 g/4½ oz. white flower modelling paste

50 g/2 oz. black fondant icing

For the meringue mushrooms

3 large/US extra-large egg whites

225 g/generous 1 cup caster/ superfine sugar

green gel or paste food colouring

red gel or paste food colouring

50 g/2 oz. dark/bittersweet chocolate, melted and left to thicken a little

edible piping gel

2 teaspoons edible confetti

2 baking sheets lined with baking parchment

3 disposable piping/pastry bags

4.5-cm/1¾-inch round pastry/ cookie cutter

wooden skewer

food-safe wire (optional)

SERVES 24

For the mushrooms, preheat the oven to 110°C (225°F) Gas ¼. Whisk the egg whites to soft peaks, add the sugar and whisk for 5–8 minutes until stiff.

Colour a serving spoonful of the meringue pastel green. Put 2–3 blobs of green meringue onto a baking sheet. Take one-third of the remaining mixture and colour it pink with red colouring. Fill a piping/pastry bag, snip a 2.5-cm/1-inch hole at the tip and pipe blobs onto the same baking sheet. Dab the points with a wet finger. For the mushroom bases, fill a second piping/pastry bag with another third of the mixture. Snip a 1.5-cm/⅝-inch hole at the tip and pipe slightly smaller blobs, leaving the points. For striped mushrooms, turn the third piping/pastry bag inside-out over a bottle. Paint stripes of red colouring down the sides, then turn it the right way. Fill with the white meringue, snip a 2.5-cm/1-inch hole at the tip and pipe blobs onto a baking sheet. Bake for 40–45 minutes until crisp. Stick the bases onto the tops (trim, if necessary) using melted chocolate. Leave upside-down to dry. Once set, dot the tops of some of the plain mushrooms with piping gel and stick on edible confetti.

If necessary, trim the tops of the cakes to make level. Sandwich together using 250 g/9 oz. of the buttercream – the bottom side of the top cake should be facing up. Place on a serving plate. Crumb-coat (see page 11) the cake using 450 g/1 lb. of the buttercream. Chill for 15 minutes. Colour 200 g/7 oz. of the remaining buttercream green. Starting from the bottom, spread the green buttercream around the sides of the cake to half-way up. Add the white buttercream above it so the sides and top are coated. Blend where the colours meet, then smooth the excess buttercream.

Trim one of the ice cream cones for the cup and wrap with 50 g/2 oz. of the pink fondant. Use a cocktail stick/toothpick to make indentations around the sides, use the trimmings to make a handle and stick on with water. Use the same technique with the remaining pink fondant and cone for the tea pot. Cut a 4.5-cm/1¾-inch round from the trimmings for the 'lid'. Attach to the 'base' of the cone. Add a handle and spout. Use one of the pink meringues to plug the open end of the cone, spray the cup and pot with edible gold spray and clear glaze spray, if using. Set aside to dry. Knead together most of the red, green, yellow and blue fondant, then use to fill the cup.

Roll out the white modelling paste to an 18-cm/7-inch square. Roll out the black fondant to an 18 x 9-cm/7 x 3½-inch rectangle and cut into 18 3-cm/ 1¼-inch squares. Create a checkerboard on the white square and drape over the cake. Insert the skewer into the cake, push the cup onto it, then add the teapot. Cover the exposed skewer with pieces of the remaining coloured fondant and add some 'splashes', using food-safe wire, if liked. Use the piping gel to stick on the mushrooms and to brush the 'tea' for a shiny effect.

Unicorn dreamer

A cake for the ultimate unicorn fan. Don't feel you need to add every element. Take your favourite toppings and let your imagination go unicorn wild!

1 quantity of Traditional Vanilla Sponge mixture (see page 14) baked in three greased and lined 18-cm/7-inch cake pans for 35–40 minutes until an inserted cocktail stick/toothpick comes out clean, then cooled

1 quantity of Classic Buttercream (see page 20)

violet, pink, orange, yellow and green gel or paste food colouring

200 g/7 oz. white chocolate

iridescent lustre

For the meringue kisses

3 UK large/US extra-large egg whites

225 g/8 oz. caster/ superfine sugar

violet, pink, orange, yellow and green gel or paste food colouring

For the unicorn bark

100 g/3½ oz. white chocolate

100 g/3½ oz. blue Candy Melts

100 g/3½ oz. pink Candy Melts

1 teaspoon iridescent sugar pearls

2 tablespoons small chocolate beans

For the unicorn horn

1 waffle ice cream cone

100 g/3½ oz. white chocolate

large disposable piping/ pastry bag

3 baking sheets lined with baking parchment

SERVES 24

To make the kisses, preheat the oven to 110°C (225°F) Gas ¼. Whisk the egg whites to soft peaks, add the sugar and whisk for 5–8 minutes until stiff.

Turn the piping/pastry bag inside-out over a bottle. Paint stripes of various food colourings down the sides of the bag. Fill the bag with the meringue, ensuring there's enough room to twist the top. Snip a 2.5-cm/1-inch hole at the tip and pipe small blobs onto two of the lined baking sheets. Bake for 40–45 minutes until crisp. Allow to cool on a wire rack.

To make the bark, melt the white chocolate and the Candy Melts each in a heatproof bowl set over a pan of simmering water (or microwave on high in 30-second bursts, stirring in between). Working quickly, spoon the white chocolate onto a lined baking sheet, then drop over spoonfuls of the blue Candy Melts and spoonfuls of the pink Candy Melts until you get a rectangle. Use a cocktail stick/toothpick to swirl the colours. Scatter over the cake sprinkles and chill until set. Break into shards and chill until needed.

To make the unicorn horn, line a small plate with baking parchment. Melt the white chocolate as above. Hold the waffle cone over the bowl, spoon over the melted chocolate and turn to coat. Stand on the lined plate. Chill until set.

If necessary, trim the tops of the cakes to make level. Sandwich together using 300 g/10½ oz. of the buttercream – the bottom side of the top cake should be facing up. Place the cake on a serving plate. Crumb-coat (see page 11) the cake using 400 g/14 oz. of the buttercream. Chill for 15 minutes.

Place 200 g/7 oz. of the buttercream into a bowl and colour it violet. Divide the remaining buttercream between four bowls. Colour one pink, one orange, one yellow, one green. Spread the pink buttercream around the base, coming 2.5 cm/1 inch up the sides. Spread an orange row above it, followed by a yellow row, green row and violet row. Smooth and remove the excess buttercream with a palette knife/metal spatula.

Meanwhile, melt the white chocolate as above. Pour the chocolate around the top of the cake, next to the edge, allowing it to trickle down the sides, then work in a spiral motion moving inwards to completely cover the top of the cake. Sweep across the top with a long palette knife/metal spatula. Working quickly, push the unicorn horn, bark and meringue kisses into the cake. Allow to set, then brush the white chocolate drips and the toppings with the iridescent lustre.

Ultra violet

1 quantity of Traditional Vanilla Sponge mixture (see page 14) baked in three greased and lined 18-cm/7-inch cake pans for 35–40 minutes until an inserted cocktail stick/toothpick comes out clean, then cooled

1 quantity of Brilliant White Buttercream (see page 21)

purple gel or paste food colouring

5 small packs of Parma Violets, crushed

1 tablespoon freeze-dried violets

25 g/1 oz. purple sugar crystals

20 g/³⁄₄ oz. silver sugar pearls

bright purple edible glitter flakes, for brushing

food-safe, pesticide-free purple and lilac violas and pansies, to decorate

soft-bristled paintbrush

food-safe wire, approx 70 cm/28 inches long

strong double-sided tape

SERVES 20

Trim the tops of the cakes to make level, if necessary. Sandwich together using 350 g/12 oz. of the buttercream – the bottom side of the top cake should be facing up. Place the cake on a serving plate or cake board. Crumb-coat (see page 11) the cake using 450 g/1 lb. of the buttercream. Place in the fridge to chill for 15 minutes.

To create an ombre effect, place 300 g/10¹⁄₂ oz. of the remaining buttercream in a bowl and set aside. Divide the remaining buttercream between two bowls, stir the purple colouring through one bowl to get a bright shade, stir a little less through the second bowl to get a lilac colour.

Using a dinner knife, starting from the bottom, spread the bright purple buttercream around the sides of the cake so that it comes to about one-third of the way up the sides (see buttercreamy tip). Add the lilac buttercream above it so two-thirds of the cake is covered, then complete the final third and top with the white buttercream so the cake is fully coated. With the knife, gently blend the buttercream where each of the colours meet, then smooth and remove the excess buttercream with a palette knife/metal spatula.

Mix the Parma Violets, freeze-dried violets and sprinkles together in a bowl (not the glitter flakes). Make two indented marks in a diagonal pattern across the sides of the cake to act as a guide. Place the cake on the cake plate onto a wire rack set over a large baking sheet and press on the sprinkles, regathering as necessary, using the indented marks as a guide. Brush with the edible glitter flakes.

An hour or so before serving, bend one end of the food-safe wire round into a 'C' shape to create a base to fit on top of the cake, then spiral the remaining wire upwards. Wrap the double-sided tape around the spiral part (the part that will not touch the cake). Stick the flowers to the spiral to cover the tape completely, then place on the top of the cake, gently pressing the base into the buttercream. Place flowers on the cake to cover the wire. The flowers are for decorative purposes only and should be removed as you cut the cake.

Buttercreamy tip:

Try not to overload your knife – it is easier to add small amounts of buttercream often rather than try to sweep large amounts across the cake.

Using flowers and petals:

See note on page 34.

Rainbow drops cake

This cake highlights what can be done with a few drops of colour! There's no need to be neat here, splodge on the icing and splatter over the colour. Great for unleashing your inner Jackson Pollock!

1 quantity of Traditional Vanilla Sponge mixture (see page 14)

1 quantity of Classic Buttercream (see page 20)

red, orange, yellow, green, blue and purple gel or paste food colouring

150 g/1 cup icing/confectioners' sugar, sifted

3 18-cm/7-inch cake pans, greased and lined

SERVES 20

Preheat the oven to 180°C (350°F) Gas 4. Divide the sponge mixture between six bowls (see cakey tip). Stir the red colouring into one bowl, the orange into one bowl, the yellow into one bowl, the green into one bowl, the blue into one bowl and the purple into the final bowl. Stir in enough colouring so you have bright vibrant colours. Pick three of the coloured batters to transfer to each of the three prepared pans (cover the remaining bowls with clingfilm/plastic wrap).

Bake for 20–25 minutes until an inserted cocktail stick/toothpick comes out clean. Allow the baked cakes to cool in the pans for 10 minutes, then remove to cool completely on a wire rack.

Wash the pans and grease and line again. Transfer the three remaining coloured batters to each of the pans and bake as above.

Trim the tops of the cakes to make level. Sandwich together using 600 g/ 1 lb. 5 oz. of the buttercream. Place the purple cake on a serving plate, then spread with some buttercream. Repeat, sandwiching on top the blue, green, yellow, orange and red cakes – the bottom side of the red cake should be facing up.

Crumb-coat (see page 11) the cake using about 450 g/1 lb. of the remaining buttercream. Place in the fridge to chill for 15 minutes, then use the remaining buttercream to coat the cake in a second layer. Using a small palette knife/metal spatula, sweep the sides in crossing motions and make small swirling motions on the top to create texture. Set aside for a few hours or overnight so the buttercream forms a crust.

To make the rainbow drop glaze, mix the icing/confectioners' sugar with about 4 teaspoons of water to make a dripping consistency thick enough to coat the back of a spoon. Divide the glaze between six bowls. Stir the red colouring into one bowl, the orange into one bowl, the yellow into one bowl, the green into one bowl, the blue into one bowl and the purple into the final bowl. Use a different teaspoon for each colour and use to drizzle and splatter the colours over the top and sides of the cake.

Cakey tip:
To make sure the layers are even, weigh the total sponge batter, then divide this figure by six. The total weight should be around 1.65 kg/3 lb. 10 oz. so each bowl should have around 275 g/9½ oz. of batter.

Modern art mirror cake

75 g/³/₄ stick butter, softened

150 g/1 cup icing/confectioners' sugar, sifted

¹/₂ quantity of Double Chocolate Sponge mixture (see page 16) baked in a greased and lined deep 20-cm/8-inch cake pan for 50 minutes until an inserted cocktail stick/ toothpick comes out clean, then cooled

For the glaze

1 UK 13-g pack/1¹/₃ US ¹/₄-oz packs gelatine powder

200 g/1 cup caster/ superfine sugar

200 g/7 oz. liquid glucose

150 g/5 oz. condensed milk

200 g/7 oz. white chocolate, 30% cocoa solids, finely chopped

blue, purple and pink gel or paste food colouring

a food thermometer (optional but helpful)

SERVES 12

For the buttercream crumb coat, beat the butter until pale and creamy, then beat in the icing/confectioners' sugar with 1–2 teaspoons of water until smooth and creamy.

Crumb-coat the cake (see page 11). This is best if the buttercream is as smooth as possible. Transfer the cake to a 20-cm/8-inch cake board or use the 20-cm/8-inch base from the cake pan (or one that is 1.5 cm/ ⁵/₈ inch smaller than the cake). Freeze the cake for at least 2 hours.

Place the chocolate in a heatproof bowl and set aside. Tip the gelatine into a small bowl and pour over 80 ml/scant ¹/₃ cup cold water. Set aside.

Put the sugar and glucose in a pan with 100 ml/¹/₃ cup water over a medium heat, stir occasionally and simmer until the sugar has dissolved. Remove from the heat and stir in the gelatine. Stir through the condensed milk. Pour the mixture over the chocolate and allow to sit for 5 minutes without stirring.

With a hand whisk, beat until smooth and shiny. Divide the chocolate mixture between four bowls; they can differ in volume as you may want one colour to be the 'main' colour and the others to be 'highlights'. Colour three bowls with the three different colourings, then use more of the purple colour in the fourth bowl so you have a lilac colour in one bowl and a deeper purple in the other. Tap the bowls on the surface to encourage any air bubbles to pop, then set aside to thicken and cool to room temperature, around 20°C/68°F. This will take a little while. Stir every so often so that the glaze doesn't start to set around the edges. Meanwhile, cover a baking sheet with clingfilm/ plastic wrap and place a cereal bowl on top.

When the glazes are at the right temperature, remove the cake from the freezer and place on top of the cereal bowl. Working fairly quickly, pour the glazes over the cake (reserving some for the top pattern) – the excess will drip onto the lined sheet. Use separate spoons for each of the reserved colours and use to drizzle or flick stripes of colour across the top of the cake. Go as subtle or wild as you like! Allow to sit for 1 hour at room temperature; you may have a few drips hanging from the bottom of the cake as it sets. It's best to snip these off with kitchen scissors. Chill for 2 hours before serving. Transfer to a serving plate or cake board.

Hugs and meringue kisses

1 quantity of Traditional Vanilla Sponge mixture (see page 14) baked in three greased and lined 18-cm/7-inch cake pans for 35–40 minutes until an inserted cocktail stick/toothpick comes out clean, then cooled

1 quantity of Classic Buttercream (see page 20)

orange gel or paste food colouring

For the meringue kisses

3 UK large/US extra-large egg whites

225 g/generous 1 cup caster/superfine sugar

orange and pink gel or paste food colouring

20 g/³/₄ oz. dark/bittersweet chocolate, melted

5 disposable piping/pastry bags

2 baking sheets lined with baking parchment

1 large star nozzle/tip

SERVES 20

To make the kisses, preheat the oven to 110°C (225°F) Gas ¼. Whisk the egg whites to soft peaks. Add the sugar and whisk for 5–8 minutes until stiff.

Place one-quarter of the mixture in a bowl, add a little orange food colouring to get a light peach shade. Use to fill a disposable piping/pastry bag. Snip a 2.5-cm/1-inch hole at the tip and pipe six small blobs on one of the lined baking sheets. Repeat with a new piping/pastry bag with some of the white meringue. Squeeze any remaining meringue back into the bowl.

Fill another piping/pastry bag fitted with the large star nozzle/tip with some of the meringue mixture and pipe seven small star shapes onto one of the lined baking sheets. Squeeze any remaining meringue back into the bowl.

For striped meringues, turn another piping/pastry bag inside-out over a bottle and paint stripes of pink colouring down the sides of the bag. Turn it back the right way, fill with half the remaining meringue, snip a 2.5-cm/1-inch hole at the tip and pipe small blobs onto the other baking sheet. Repeat with the orange colouring and remaining meringue using another piping/pastry bag.

Bake the meringues for 40–45 minutes or until crisp. Allow to cool on a wire rack. Drizzle some of the white 'blob' meringues with the melted chocolate.

If necessary, trim the tops of the cakes to make level. Remove 75 g/2³/₄ oz. of the buttercream and colour it a light peach shade. Cover and set aside. Sandwich the cakes together using 350 g/12 oz. of the remaining buttercream – the bottom side of the top cake should be facing up. Place the cake on a serving plate or cake board. Crumb-coat (see page 11) the cake using 450 g/1 lb. of the remaining buttercream. Place in the fridge for 15 minutes, then use the remaining buttercream to coat the cake in a second layer. Smooth and remove the excess buttercream with a palette knife/metal spatula (reserve the excess buttercream). Smear small blobs of the reserved peach buttercream around the cake with a dinner knife, then smooth and remove the excess buttercream once more to spread the peach colour.

Pile some of the meringue kisses on top of the cake to one side (use a little of the reserved excess buttercream to secure in place, if necessary), then use the meringue kisses to decorate the front side of the cake in a curved 'sweeping' pattern – if the buttercream has formed a crust, brush the spots you want to stick the meringues to with a little water.

1 quantity of Traditional Vanilla
  Sponge mixture (see page 14)
  baked in three greased and
  lined 18-cm/7-inch cake pans
  for 35–40 minutes until an
  inserted cocktail stick/toothpick
  comes out clean, then cooled

1.8 kg/4 lb. Classic Buttercream
  (see page 20 with quantities:
  350 g/3 sticks unsalted butter,
  250 g/1¼ cups vegetable fat,
  1.2 kg/8½ cups icing/
  confectioners' sugar and
  2–3 tablespoons water)

turquoise gel or paste
  food colouring

100 g/3½ oz. edible
  ocean-coloured pearls

edible silver spray

75 g/2½ oz. clear mint hard-
  boiled sweets/hard candies

For the mermaid tails

50 g/2 oz. white flower
  modelling paste

50 g/2 oz. orange flower
  modelling paste

50 g/2 oz. turquoise flower
  modelling paste

25 g/1 oz. red flower
  modelling paste

1 tablespoon icing/confectioners'
  sugar, plus extra for dusting

3 ice cream cones (with a sharp
  knife, use a gentle sawing
  motion to cut off the flared
  tops – cut 1 or 2 at a slight
  angle)

1 tablespoon edible gold confetti

edible glue or piping gel

*2 baking sheets lined with
  baking parchment*

*disposable piping/pastry bag fitted
  with a large round nozzle/tip*

SERVES 20

Mermaid cake

Who doesn't want to be a mermaid?
A cake for those who want to make a splash!

For the mermaid tails, knead the white and coloured modelling pastes separately until malleable, then knead together briefly so the colours intertwine. Roll out thinly on a surface dusted with icing/confectioners' sugar and cut out three triangles wide enough to wrap around the ice cream cones. Gently press to seal. Brush with edible glue or piping gel and scatter with gold confetti. Cut out three smaller triangles, 9 cm/3½ inch wide at the base and 7 cm/2¾ inch on the remaining two sides. Roll the end of a cocktail stick/toothpick along the bases so they curl up. Press the cocktail stick/toothpick onto the main body of each triangle so the indentation marks look like markings on a fin. Place on a lined baking sheet and drape over wooden spoon handles. Allow to dry overnight along with the covered cones.

Mix the icing/confectioners' sugar with a few drops of water to form a thick, glue-like paste. Use to stick the 'fins' to the 'tails'. Let dry for at least 4 hours.

If necessary, trim the tops of the cakes to make level. Sandwich together using 350 g/12 oz. of the buttercream – the bottom side of the top cake should be facing up. Place the cake on a serving plate. Crumb-coat (see page 11) the cake using 450 g/1 lb. of the buttercream. Colour the rest of the buttercream bright turquoise. Place in the fridge for 15 minutes, then use 600 g/1 lb. 5 oz. of the buttercream to coat the cake in a second layer. Smooth and remove the excess buttercream with a palette knife/metal spatula. Use some of the excess buttercream to decorate the top in a wave-like pattern.

Make a diagonal indentation across the front of the cake with a ruler. Mirror this on the back of the cake. Make a vertical mark with a knife to make two sections below the diagonal line. Place the cake on the board onto a wire rack set over a baking sheet and press the ocean-coloured pearls onto one side of the cake using the indented marks as a guide.

Fill the piping/pastry bag fitted with a large round nozzle/tip with the rest of the turquoise buttercream. Working above, but following, the long diagonal line, pipe blobs of buttercream. Start at the base of the cake and work towards the top. As you pipe each blob, drag across slightly as you pull away. You will need to pipe the 'front' of the cake and then repeat for the 'back'. Spray the cake with edible silver spray. Position the mermaid tails on top.

In a mini food processor, process the sweets/candies to a sugar-like consistency. Place in a small saucepan and gently heat until melted. Spoon small blobs onto a lined baking sheet, then use the back of a spoon to spread the blobs into splash-like shapes. Once set, insert into the cake.

MAGICAL DAYS OUT

Film lover cake

All that's great about going to the cinema on a cake –
what more could you want?!

1 quantity of Traditional Vanilla
   Sponge mixture (see page 14)
   baked in three greased and
   lined 18-cm/7-inch cake
   pans for 35–40 minutes until
   an inserted cocktail stick/
   toothpick comes out clean,
   then cooled

1 quantity of Classic
   Buttercream (see page 20)

100 g/3$\frac{1}{2}$ oz. toffee popcorn

100 g/$\frac{1}{2}$ cup caster/
   superfine sugar

handful of salted pretzels

5 red liquorice/licorice sticks,
   such as Red Vines

3 peanut butter cups,
   such as Reese's

1 chocolate-coated caramel bar,
   such as a Curly Wurly,
   cut into two pieces

readymade toffee sauce,
   for drizzling

For the popcorn bag bark

125 g/4$\frac{1}{2}$ oz. white chocolate,
   chopped, or white Candy
   Melts

75 g/2$\frac{1}{2}$ oz. red Candy Melts
   (see chocolatey tip)

disposable piping/pastry bag

SERVES 24

For the popcorn bag bark, place a square of baking parchment on the work surface. Melt the white chocolate or Candy Melts (see chocolatey tip) in a heatproof bowl set over a pan of simmering water (or microwave on high in 30 second bursts, stirring in between). Spoon the chocolate onto the baking parchment and spread out with a palette knife/metal spatula to a rectangle about 21 x 14 cm/8$\frac{1}{2}$ x 5$\frac{1}{2}$ inches. Gently wiggle the baking parchment to smooth the top. Allow to set for 3–5 minutes until it has thickened but is not hard.

Place a rolling pin and a wooden spoon on a baking sheet, then slide the chocolate-coated parchment over them to create a wave effect. Chill until set. Melt the red Candy Melts as above. Spoon into the piping/pastry bag, snip off the end and pipe downwards stripes along the chocolate rectangle. Allow to set.

If necessary, trim the tops of the cakes to make level. Sandwich together using 350 g/12 oz. of the buttercream – the bottom side of the top cake should be facing up. Place the cake on a serving plate or cake board.

Crumb-coat (see page 11) the cake using 450 g/1 lb. of the buttercream. Place in the fridge for 15 minutes, then use the remaining buttercream to coat the cake in a second layer. Smooth and remove the excess buttercream with a palette knife/metal spatula. Gently press a layer of popcorn onto one-quarter of the top of the cake to make a base for the tower of popcorn.

Place the sugar in a dry pan and gently heat, gently shaking the pan occasionally, until melted. Use as a glue to make the tower of popcorn on top of the popcorn base. Be careful as it will be very hot (you may need to re-melt if it starts to set again). Add in a few pretzels as you go.

Push the popcorn bag bark, liquorice/licorice sticks, peanut butter cups, chocolate-coated caramel bar and remaining pretzels into the top of cake around the popcorn. Drizzle with the toffee sauce just before serving.

Chocolatey tip:
If using Candy Melts, they may need thinning a little – after melting, stir through a little vegetable fat, if necessary, such as Trex or Cookeen.

Fairground fun cake

All the fun of the fair – I nearly bought a few golf tees and added on some mini chocolate eggs for a coconut shy, but thought I had to rein it in at some point! Go for a combination of your fairground favourites.

1 quantity of Traditional Vanilla Sponge mixture (see page 14)

red and green gel or paste food colouring

1.2 kg/2 lb. 10 oz. Classic Buttercream (see page 20, with quantities: 250 g/ 2¼ sticks unsalted butter, 150 g/5 oz. vegetable fat and 800 g/5¾ cups icing/ confectioners' sugar)

½ quantity of Royal Icing (see page 22)

40 g/generous ½ cup desiccated/dried unsweetened shredded coconut

3 large striped lolly pops

2 small striped lolly pops

2–3 small rubber ducks

chocolate gold coins, to decorate

mini bunting (optional, see crafty tip)

12-hole cake pop mould, greased with sunflower oil

2 deep 20-cm/8-inch cake pans, greased and lined

disposable piping/pastry bag fitted with a small round nozzle/tip

SERVES 20

Preheat the oven to 180°C (350°F) Gas 4.

First make the cake pops for the dotty sponge. Place 275 g/9½ oz. of the cake batter into a bowl (cover the remaining batter with a damp, clean kitchen towel) and colour bright red. Spoon the red batter into the greased cake pop mould (you will need to bake in batches). You should get around 36 cake pops. Place on a baking sheet. Bake for 10 minutes, cool in the mould for 5 minutes, then remove and leave to cool on a wire rack.

Add the cake pops to the reserved cake mixture and stir with a wooden spoon. Divide the mixture between the two cake pans. Bake for 40–45 minutes until an inserted cocktail stick/toothpick comes out clean. Cool in the pans for 10 minutes, then turn out and cool completely on a wire rack.

If necessary, trim the tops of the cakes to make level. Sandwich together using 250 g/9 oz. of the buttercream – the bottom side of the top cake should be facing up. Place the cake on a serving plate or cake board. Crumb-coat (see page 11) the cake using 450 g/1 lb. of the buttercream. Place in the fridge for 15 minutes, then use the remaining buttercream to coat the cake in a second layer. Smooth and remove the excess buttercream with a palette knife/metal spatula.

Add enough red colouring to the royal icing to get a bright colour. Use to fill the piping/pastry bag fitted with the small round nozzle/tip. Pipe stripes around the sides – start from the top, drawing the icing down to the base, finishing with a little 'pearl' at the bottom. Allow to set.

In a small bowl, stir a dot of green colouring into a little water, add the desiccated/dried unsweetened shredded coconut and mix until it turns green. Sprinkle over the top of the cake. Insert the lolly pops, then add the rubber ducks and chocolate gold coins. Insert the bunting, if using. Remove any inedible decorations before slicing.

Crafty tip:

To make bunting, fold strips of colourful paper or card in half, cut out small triangles (so the top edge is along the fold), unfold and glue near the points, then press back together. Thread onto a piece of string/twine. Insert two wooden skewers into the cake and secure the bunting in place with double-sided sticky tape.

Watercolour washout

I love making one statement flower – you can make this one without any fancy equipment and it gives real show-stopping results. This lily shape also looks fab on this watercolour-style back-drop.

pink, green, lilac and bright blue gel or paste food colouring

60 g/2¼ oz. white flower modelling paste

2 teaspoons runny honey

edible gold glitter

1.75 kg/3 lb 14 oz. Classic Buttercream (see page 20, with quantities: 350 g/ 3 sticks unsalted butter, 250 g/1¼ cups vegetable fat and 1.15 kg/8 cups icing/ confectioners' sugar)

edible gold spray (optional)

1 quantity of Traditional Vanilla Sponge mixture (see page 14) baked in three greased and lined 18-cm/7-inch cake pans for 35–40 minutes until an inserted cocktail stick/ toothpick comes out clean, then cooled

200 g/7 oz. white chocolate, chopped

2 bay leaves

pale silver edible lustre

pale blue edible lustre

disposable piping/pastry bag

soft-bristled paintbrush

SERVES 20

To make the flower, dot a little pink colouring onto the flower modelling paste and knead well. Roll one-third into seven pea-sized balls. Roll them as thin as possible on baking parchment, to create seven long petal shapes. Drape over the base of an upturned shot glass so the ends overlap and press the ends together with a little water. Bend the lengths slightly to give them a floaty shape. Roll the remaining flower paste in the same way into ten thin sausage-shaped petals. Drape over the base of a deep, upturned cereal bowl and press the ends together with a little water. Leave to set overnight.

Once set, remove the petals from the glass and bowl and invert. Brush the edges of the petals with the honey and scatter over the gold glitter, gently brushing off the excess. Put a little blob of buttercream in the centre of the larger flower and gently nestle the smaller flower inside. Fill the piping/pastry bag with 50 g/2 oz. of the buttercream. Snip a small hole in the end and pipe little 'spikes' in the centre of the flower. Spray with edible gold spray, if using.

If necessary, trim the tops of the cakes to make level. Sandwich together using 350 g/12 oz. of the buttercream – the bottom side of the top cake should be facing up. Place the cake on a serving plate or cake board. Crumb-coat (see page 11) the cake using 450 g/1 lb. of the buttercream. Chill for 15 minutes.

Place 550 g/19 oz. of buttercream in a bowl and colour it pale green. Use to coat the cake in a second layer. Smooth and remove the excess buttercream with a palette knife/metal spatula. Divide the remaining buttercream between four bowls. Stir green colouring into one bowl, lilac into the second, pink into the third and blue into the fourth to get a bright blue.

Use a different dinner knife for each colour and smear small blobs of each colour around the cake. Smooth and remove the excess buttercream once more to spread the colours (you may not use all of each of the colours – use them like an artist's palette and use more or less of the colours, as desired).

Melt the white chocolate in a heatproof bowl set over a pan of simmering water (or microwave on high in 30-second bursts, stirring in between). Pour the melted chocolate around the edge of the top of the cake, allowing it to trickle down the sides. Continue drizzling the chocolate in a spiral motion moving inwards to cover the top of the cake. Gently smooth the top with a palette knife/metal spatula. Position the waterlily and bay leaves on top. Let set, then brush with the silver and blue lustres. Use a warmed knife to cut.

Seaside breeze

1 quantity of Traditional Vanilla Sponge mixture (see page 14)

3 flat-based ice cream cones

75 g/2½ oz. digestive biscuits/graham crackers, crushed

25 g/2 tablespoons butter, melted

1.8 kg/4 lb. Two-ingredient Buttercream (see page 20, with quantities: 600 g/5¼ sticks butter, 1.2 kg/8½ cups icing/confectioners' sugar and 2–3 tablespoons water)

1 quantity of Royal Icing (see page 22)

blue gel or paste food colouring

75 g/2½ oz. white chocolate, melted

chocolate writing icing

2–3 Flake pieces

1 teaspoon ice cream sprinkles

3 18-cm/7-inch cake pans, greased and lined

hair dryer (with a cool setting)

wooden skewer

disposable piping/pastry bag fitted with a large star nozzle/tip

SERVES 22

Preheat the oven to 180°C (350°F) Gas 4.

Divide 6 tablespoons of the cake batter between the three flat-based ice cream cones. Bake for 20 minutes and cool on a wire rack. Divide the remaining batter between the cake pans. Bake for 35–40 minutes until an inserted cocktail stick/toothpick comes out clean. Allow to cool in the pans for 10 minutes, then remove and place on a wire rack to cool completely.

Stir the crushed digestive biscuits/graham crackers into the melted butter. Allow to cool.

If necessary, trim the tops of the cakes to make level. Sandwich together using 350 g/12 oz. of the buttercream – the bottom side of the top cake should be facing up. Place the cake on a serving plate or cake board. Crumb-coat (see page 11) the cake using 450 g/1 lb. of the buttercream. Place in the fridge to chill for 15 minutes.

Break up the cooled biscuit/cracker crumbs with a wooden spoon, if necessary. Put into a bowl with 750 g/1 lb. 10 oz. of the remaining buttercream. Use an electric hand whisk to combine. Use to coat the cake in a thick second layer. Smooth and remove the excess buttercream with a palette knife/metal spatula (cover the remaining buttercream with clingfilm/plastic wrap).

With the hair dryer at the ready on a cool setting, colour the royal icing mid-bright blue. Add a few drops of water to thin, if necessary – you need a thick but free-flowing consistency. Spoon most of the icing over the top of the cake, then use a palette knife/metal spatula to ease the icing over the sides. Blast with the hair dryer as it trickles down to create a wind-swept look. Use a spoon to flick the remaining icing across the cake in the same direction to enhance the dramatic effect. Insert the skewer into the top of the cake (where the upright ice cream cone will be). Allow to dry overnight.

Whisk the remaining buttercream to a smooth piping consistency, adding a few drops of water, if necessary. Use to fill the disposable piping/pastry bag fitted with the large star nozzle/tip. Pipe swirls on the top of the ice cream cones. Place spoonfuls of the melted white chocolate on the top of the cake, then position two of the cones in a 'falling' position on top. Push the third cone standing upright onto the skewer and drizzle with a little melted chocolate to create a 'dripping' effect. Decorate the ice creams with the writing icing, Flake pieces and ice cream sprinkles.

High drama

icing/confectioners' sugar, for dusting

45 g/1¾ oz. gold flower modelling paste

115 g/4 oz. red flower modelling paste

edible piping gel, for brushing

1 teaspoon each edible gold and red glitter, plus extra for finishing touches

1 quantity of Double Chocolate Sponge mixture (see page 16) baked in three greased and lined 18-cm/7-inch cake pans for 40 minutes until an inserted cocktail stick/toothpick comes out clean, then cooled

1 quantity of Classic Buttercream (see page 20)

orange and yellow gel or paste food colouring

75 g/2½ oz. black fondant icing

200 g/7 oz. red fondant icing

200 g/7 oz. brown or chocolate-flavoured fondant icing

55 g/2 oz. white flower modelling paste

10 yellow peanut M&M's

2 Oreo cookies

3–4 star cutters ranging in size from 3–5 cm/1–2 inches

10-cm/4-inch round pastry/cookie cutter

2 cocktail sticks/toothpicks

8–10 thin wooden skewers, cut to different lengths

SERVES 20

On a surface dusted with icing/confectioners' sugar, roll out 40 g/1½ oz. of the gold modelling paste and 40 g/1½ oz. of the red modelling paste to 4 mm/⅛ inch thick. Stamp out 4–5 of each colour using the cutters. Set aside. Brush with piping gel and coat in the corresponding glitter.

If necessary, trim the tops of the cakes to make level. Sandwich together using 350 g/12 oz. of the buttercream – the bottom side of the top cake should be facing up. Place the cake on a serving plate. Remove 50 g/2 oz. of the remaining buttercream and colour it orange. Cover and set aside.

Crumb-coat (see page 11) the cake using 450 g/1 lb. of the buttercream. Chill for 15 minutes. Colour the remaining buttercream yellow. Use to coat the cake in a second layer. Smooth and remove the excess buttercream with a palette knife/metal spatula. Smear blobs of the reserved orange buttercream around the top half of the cake with a dinner knife; smooth to blend.

Roll out 50 g/2 oz. of the black fondant and slide onto a chopping board. Use a sharp knife to cut out three silhouette head shapes, 5–7.5 cm/2–3 inches high. Attach to the front of the cake at the base using a little water. For the 'curtains', roll out the red fondant to two 17-cm/6¾-inch squares, cut each into strips of varying widths from 1–2.5 cm/⅜–1 inch, and stick lengthways next to the silhouettes and around the sides and back of the cake, leaving little gaps between each strip. Trim, if necessary.

Roll out the remaining red modelling paste as thin as possible. Stamp out two 10-cm/4-inch rounds. Cut the top one-third off each round so you have four pieces. Stick the larger semi-circles to the cake above the silhouettes, and shape into curtain-like pleats. Repeat with the small semi-circles. Once hardened slightly, brush the edges with piping gel and gold glitter. Use the remaining 5 g/¼ oz. of gold modelling paste to create a 'cord' and stick it where the semi-circles meet. Brush with piping gel and gold glitter.

Roll out the brown fondant to a rough 10-cm/4-inch circle. Tear 40 g/1½ oz. of the white modelling paste into pieces, scatter over the circle, knead briefly and roll out to a 19-cm/7½-inch circle. Cut into strips 2 cm/¾ inch wide. Stick to the top of the cake to make floorboards. Make indentations with a knife and snip the ends with scissors. For the 'spotlights', roll the remaining black fondant into a long 1 cm/⅜ inch thick sausage and cut into ten 1-cm/⅜-inch pieces. Attach to the outside edge of the 'floorboards' with piping gel, leaving a space front-right. Stick an M&M on top of each with piping gel. Roll out the remaining 15 g/½ oz. of white modelling paste thinly. Cut out masks of 'Comedy' and 'Tragedy', 3.5 cm/1½ inches high. Attach to the Oreos with piping gel, then attach to the cake using the cocktail sticks/toothpicks. Attach the stars to the cake using the skewers.

Glam rock cake

1 quantity of Traditional Vanilla Sponge mixture (see page 14)

75 g/2^{1}/$_{2}$ oz. dark/bittersweet chocolate, melted

1^{1}/$_{2}$ tablespoons unsweetened cocoa powder mixed with 2 tablespoons just-boiled water

black gel or paste food colouring (optional)

^{1}/$_{4}$ quantity of Two-ingredient Buttercream (see page 20)

^{2}/$_{3}$ quantity of Glossy Black Fudge Icing (see page 23)

icing/confectioners' sugar, for dusting

250 g/9 oz. white fondant icing

1^{1}/$_{2}$ tablespoons thick mixed coloured sugar strands

1^{1}/$_{2}$ tablespoons multi-coloured star sprinkles

1^{1}/$_{2}$ tablespoons small silver sugar balls

15–20 large silver sugar balls

2–3 liquorice/licorice Catherine Wheels

For the glam rock bark

100 g/3^{1}/$_{2}$ oz. dark/bittersweet chocolate

12–14 edible gold gems

1 teaspoon multi-coloured star sprinkles

For the lightening strike

100 g/3^{1}/$_{2}$ oz. red Candy Melts

^{1}/$_{2}$ teaspoon small orange and yellow sprinkles

3 18-cm/7-inch cake pans, greased and lined

baking sheet lined with baking parchment

2 disposable piping/pastry bags

1 large star nozzle/tip

SERVES 20

This glossy frosting was just calling out for a studded leather-look and surprise-inside animal print sponge.

Preheat the oven to 180°C (350°F) Gas 4.

Divide the sponge mixture between two bowls. Fold the melted chocolate and cocoa powder mix through one bowl until incorporated. Stir through the black colouring, if using, to get a dark brown-black colour. Drop alternate spoonfuls of the mixes between the three cake pans. Swirl the mix in each pan with a cocktail stick/toothpick, then tap the pans on the surface to level the mixture. Bake for 35–40 minutes until an inserted cocktail stick/toothpick comes out clean. Cool in the pans for 10 minutes, then turn out onto a wire rack to cool completely. If necessary, trim the tops of the cakes to make level.

To make the glam rock bark, melt the chocolate in a heatproof bowl set over a pan of simmering water (or microwave on high in 30 second bursts, stirring in between). Drizzle onto the lined baking sheet and use the back of a spoon to ease the chocolate to a 14-cm/5^{1}/$_{2}$-inch square. Gently wiggle the paper to level the surface, leave to set for a few minutes, then stick the gold gems to one side of the square and scatter the multi-coloured star sprinkles over the other side. Chill until set. Break into shards and chill until needed.

Draw a lightening strike, 20 x 7 cm/8 x 3 inches, on baking parchment. Turn over and place onto a baking sheet. Melt the red Candy Melts as above. Fill a piping/pastry bag, snip a small hole in the tip and follow the outline of the lightening. Fill the outline, then wiggle the paper to level the surface. Let set for a few minutes, scatter over the orange and yellow sprinkles and chill.

Sandwich the cakes together using the buttercream – the bottom side of the top cake should be facing up. Place the cake on a serving plate. Reserve 150 g/5 oz. of the glossy black icing, then crumb-coat (see page 11) the cake using some of the remaining glossy black icing. Chill for 15 minutes.

On a work surface lightly dusted with icing/confectioners' sugar, roll out the fondant to 3 mm/^{1}/$_{8}$ inch thickness. Use the base of the cake pan to cut out a circle. Lay half of the circle on the top of the cake, allowing the other half to rest on the side, gently smoothing into position.

Use the rest of the black icing to coat the black part of the cake liberally in a thick second layer. Mix the sugar strands with the star sprinkles and small silver balls. Press them onto the base section of the icing. Add the large silver balls around the side near the top. Fill a piping/pastry bag fitted with the large star nozzle/tip with the reserved icing and pipe little swirls on the cake. Add pieces of bark, the Catherine wheels and lightening strike.

Butterfly ball cake

Inspiration can come from anywhere. The idea for this cake was sparked by a fabulous orangey-pink ombre floral dress from a designer fashion collection. There are lots of small edible sugar flowers now available in supermarkets – mix them with real, food-safe, pesticide-free roses for a fast way to couture cakery.

1 quantity of Traditional Vanilla Sponge mixture (see page 14) baked in three greased and lined 18-cm/7-inch cake pans for 35–40 minutes until an inserted cocktail stick/ toothpick comes out clean, then cooled

1 quantity of Classic Buttercream (see page 20)

orange and pink gel or paste food colouring

5 silk or feather butterflies

3 readymade macarons

5–6 food-safe, pesticide-free pink and/or orange roses

10–12 readymade sugar roses

olive leaves or bay leaves

edible gold spray

food-safe wire (see crafty tip)

SERVES 20

Trim the tops of the cakes to make level, if necessary. Sandwich together using 350 g/12 oz. of the buttercream – the bottom side of the top cake should be facing up. Place the cake on a serving plate or cake board. Crumb-coat the cake (see page 11) using 400 g/14 oz. of the buttercream. Place in the fridge to chill for 15 minutes.

To create an ombre effect, place 250 g/9 oz. of the remaining buttercream into a bowl and stir through the orange colouring to get a bright shade. Stir the pink colouring through the remaining 500 g/1 lb. 2 oz. of buttercream to get a bright pink shade.

Using a dinner knife, starting from the bottom, spread the orange buttercream around the sides of the cake so that it comes to about half-way up the sides. Spread the pink buttercream above it so the sides and top are fully coated. With the tip of the knife, gently mix where the two colours meet. Smooth and remove the excess buttercream with a palette knife/metal spatula.

Wind the food-safe wire around the butterflies and insert into the top of the cake, then decorate with the macarons and fresh roses. The roses are for decorative purposes only and should be removed as you cut the cake. Decorate one side of the cake with the edible sugar flowers and olive leaves or bay leaves. Spray the whole cake with edible gold spray.

Crafty tip:

If you can't find food-safe wire, you can use ordinary thin wire, but to ensure that it doesn't come into contact with the cake, insert a thin straw into the cake, then thread the wire into the straw.

For gluten-free:

Use 1 quantity of Gluten-free Vanilla Sponge mixture (see page 15) baked in three 18-cm/7-inch cake pans for 35–40 minutes until an inserted cocktail stick/toothpick comes out clean. Check the ingredients on individual manufacturers for readymade macarons and sugar flowers.

Using flowers and petals:

See note on page 34.

Wimbledon tennis towers

A great way to ace a day at the Tennis, why not top it off with a Tennis Tower cake?
And if you didn't get tickets, it'll make watching it on TV that much sweeter.

25 g/1 oz. lime-coloured flower modelling paste

25 g/1 oz. white flower modelling paste

½ quantity of Traditional Vanilla Sponge mixture (see page 14) baked in a greased and lined 20-cm/8-inch square loose-bottomed cake pan for 35–40 minutes until an inserted cocktail stick/toothpick comes out clean, then cooled

75 g/¾ stick butter, softened

150 g/1 cup icing/confectioners' sugar, sifted, plus 3 tablespoons for the filling and extra for dusting

green gel or paste food colouring

175 ml/¾ cup double/heavy cream

2 tablespoons Pimm's

150 g/1½ cups strawberries, hulled and finely sliced

small handful of mint, torn

1 satsuma, peeled, segmented and sliced

6-cm/2½-inch pastry/cookie cutter

disposable piping/pastry bag fitted with a small star nozzle/tip

MAKES 9

Roll the lime-coloured modelling paste into nine balls. Roll 5 g/scant ¼ oz. of the white modelling paste into a very thin sausage shape, and use to add 'tennis-ball' detail to each one. Brush with a little water to attach to the balls.

Mark out nine 6-cm/2½-inch rounds using the pastry/cookie cutter on the top of the sponge – gently press into the top of the cake. Use a thin, sharp knife to follow the marks and cut out small round cakes. Transfer the cakes to the freezer for 20 minutes (this will make it easier to cut them into layers).

Meanwhile, prepare the buttercream for the topping. Beat the butter until pale and creamy, then beat in the 150 g/1 cup icing/confectioners' sugar with 2 teaspoons of water until smooth and creamy. Stir through enough green colouring to get a mid-green shade.

Remove the cakes from the freezer and cut each twice horizontally to make three layers. Decorate the top layer first. Fill the piping/pastry bag fitted with the small star nozzle/tip with the green buttercream and pipe small star shapes to completely cover the top of each one.

On a work surface lightly dusted with icing/confectioners' sugar, roll out the remaining white flower modelling paste to as thin as you can get it and cut out 18 thin strips (approximately 5 mm/¼ inch wide). Use to decorate the 'grass' tops of the cakes with 'court lines'. Trim to fit.

To make the filling, whip the cream with the remaining 3 tablespoons of icing/confectioners' sugar and the Pimm's until medium peaks form. Sandwich the cake layers together with the Pimm's cream filling, strawberries, mint and satsuma slices. Chill until ready to serve.

For gluten-free:

Use ½ quantity of Gluten-free Vanilla Sponge mixture (see page 15) baked in a 20-cm/8-inch square loose-bottomed cake pan for 35–40 minutes until an inserted cocktail stick/toothpick comes out clean. Allow to cool. Check the ingredients on individual manufacturer's packers for readymade fondant and flower modelling pastes to ensure they are gluten-free.

Super hero cake

1 quantity of Traditional Vanilla Sponge mixture (see page 14) baked in three greased and lined 18-cm/7-inch cake pans for 35–40 minutes until an inserted cocktail stick/toothpick comes out clean, then cooled

1 quantity of Classic Buttercream (see page 20)

pink, orange, blue and black gel or paste food colouring

icing/confectioners' sugar, for dusting

50 g/2 oz. black fondant icing

1 teaspoon yellow sugar pearls

150 g/5 oz. each blue and red fondant icing

75 g/2½ oz. red flower modelling paste

edible clear glaze spray (optional)

black writing icing

For the speech bubbles

100 g/7 tablespoons butter

100 g/½ cup soft brown sugar

1 egg, beaten

few drops of pure vanilla extract

275 g/2 cups plain/all-purpose flour, plus extra for dusting

1–2 teaspoons milk, if needed

50 g/2 oz. each yellow, white, red and blue fondant icing

34-g/1-oz. pack chocolate letters

edible piping gel, for brushing

4 wooden skewers

2 baking sheets lined with baking parchment

SERVES 20

For the speech bubbles, cream the butter and brown sugar together with an electric hand whisk. Stir through the egg and vanilla extract. Sift over the flour and bring the mixture together, adding the milk, if needed. Turn out onto a lightly floured surface, knead briefly and press into a ball of dough. Wrap in clingfilm/plastic wrap and place in the freezer for 30 minutes to chill.

Roll out the dough out to 4 mm/⅛–¼ inch thickness. Using a sharp knife, cut out 16–18 geometric and starburst shapes approximately 8 x 6 cm/3¼ x 2¼ inches. Insert skewers into four of the cookies (you will not need all the cookies for the cake). Place on the lined baking sheets. Chill for 30 minutes. Meanwhile, preheat the oven to 180°C (350°F) Gas 4. Bake for 12–14 minutes until just golden. Transfer to a wire rack to cool completely.

On a surface dusted with icing/confectioners' sugar, roll out the 50 g/2 oz. each of yellow, white, red and blue fondant on baking parchment as thin as possible. Brush all the skewered cookies and 1–2 of the plain cookies with a little water. Drape a piece of the fondant over the cookies to cover, then trim to fit. Cut out a smaller shape in another colour to stick on top, if liked. Use piping gel to stick chocolate letters to the cookies.

If necessary, trim the tops of the cakes to make level. Sandwich together using 350 g/12 oz. of the buttercream – the bottom side of the top cake should be facing up. Place the cake on a cake board. Crumb-coat (see page 11) the cake using 400 g/14 oz. of the buttercream. Chill for 15 minutes.

Colour 250 g/9 oz. of the remaining buttercream with the pink and orange colouring to get a bright shade. Stir the blue and black colouring through the remaining 500 g/1 lb. 2 oz. of buttercream to get a dark blue shade. Spread the pinky-orange buttercream around the base of the cake so that it comes half-way up the sides. Add the blue icing above it so the sides and top are coated. Blend where the two colours meet, then smooth over.

Create small shapes from the black fondant to create a skyline and press onto the cake. Stick on the sugar pearls for windows. Roll out the blue fondant to an 18 x 24-cm/7 x 9½-inch rectangle. Measure 9 cm/3½ inches from the top of the longest side and cut into a point. Position the point in the middle of the top of the cake and gently press the length down the left-hand side of the cake next to the skyline. Repeat to the right of the skyline with the red fondant.

Roll out the red modelling paste to a 12 x 20-cm/4¾ x 8-inch rectangle. Gather together at the shortest side to create a 'cape-effect' and attach to the cake. Spray with clear glaze, if using. Use the writing icing to pipe a web pattern on the red fondant. Spray with clear glaze spray, if using. Add the cookies.

DECADENT DIVAS

Couture stiletto cupcakes

A girl can never have too many pairs of shoes!

200 g/7 oz. white chocolate

12 sweet finger biscuits/cookies, such as Rich Tea Fingers

edible silver lustre

edible gold glitter spray

¼ quantity of Traditional Vanilla Sponge mixture (see page 14) baked in 12 cupcake cases in a muffin pan for 18–20 minutes until an inserted cocktail stick/toothpick comes out clean, then cooled

½ quantity of Classic Buttercream (see page 20)

pink gel or paste food colouring

6 sugar roses

1 tablespoon large edible sugar pearls

12 chocolate wafer rolls

baking sheet, lined with baking parchment

soft-bristled paintbrush

2 disposable piping/pastry bags

large star nozzle/tip

MAKES 12

Melt 150 g/5 oz. of the chocolate in a heatproof bowl set over a pan of simmering water (or microwave on high in 30-second bursts, stirring in between). Spread the chocolate over the top of each biscuit/cookie, leaving 1 cm/³⁄₈ inch uncovered at the end, allowing the excess to drip back into the bowl. Place the biscuits/cookies on the lined baking sheet and put in the fridge to set. Brush with silver lustre and spray with the edible glitter spray.

If necessary, trim the tops of the cakes to make level. Divide the buttercream equally between two bowls. Colour one portion pink, leave the second bowl plain. Spread a little of the pink buttercream over the top of six of the cakes. Repeat with the plain buttercream and the remaining six cakes. Spoon the remaining pink buttercream into a piping/pastry bag fitted with the large star nozzle/tip and pipe stars and/or swirls onto six of the cakes. Repeat with the remaining cakes and plain buttercream, using the second piping/pastry bag and the cleaned nozzle/tip. Decorate each 'shoe' with cake decorations.

Gently push the uncovered end of the white chocolate biscuits into the buttercream and slightly into the cakes. To create the stiletto heels, melt the remaining 50 g/2 oz. white chocolate as before, cut the wafer rolls at an angle to make sure they sit flush against the biscuit shoes and the work surface, brush with the silver lustre and spray with the gold glitter spray, then attach to the undersides of the biscuits/cookies using the melted chocolate. Leave to set.

Sultry salted caramel

Epic vegan cake anyone? This sweet, salty, caramel number hits all the right flavour notes.

1 quantity of Vegan Chocolate Sponge mixture (see page 19) baked in three greased and lined 18-cm/7-inch cake pans for 30–35 minutes until an inserted cocktail stick/toothpick comes out clean, then cooled

½ quantity of Brilliant White Buttercream (see page 21, but replace the water with 2 tablespoons of the vegan salted caramel sauce)

2 teaspoons mixed gold, silver and bronze cake sprinkles (optional, see vegan tip)

2 teaspoons rock sea salt

200 g/1 cup caster/superfine sugar

5–6 blackberries

few sprigs of lemon thyme

edible gold spray (optional, see vegan tip)

For the vegan salted caramel sauce

250 g/1¼ cups caster/superfine sugar

150 ml/⅔ cup coconut milk

2 tablespoons cornflour/cornstarch

rock sea salt, to taste

baking sheet, greased with sunflower oil

SERVES 20

For the vegan salted caramel sauce, place the sugar in a saucepan with 4 tablespoons of water, place over a medium heat, stirring occasionally, until the sugar has dissolved. Simmer for 5 minutes. Remove from the heat and stir through the coconut milk (be careful as it will bubble). Return to the heat, mix the cornflour/cornstarch with 4 tablespoons of water and stir in to the pan, simmer for a further 5–7 minutes until thickened. It will thicken further on cooling. Add salt to taste. Set aside to cool completely (see cook's tip).

If necessary, trim the tops of the cakes to make level. Sandwich together using 350 g/12 oz. of the buttercream – the bottom side of the top cake should be facing up. Place the cake on a serving plate. Crumb-coat (see page 11) the cake using the remaining buttercream. Smooth and remove the excess buttercream with a palette knife/metal spatula.

Mix the cake sprinkles (if using) with the 2 teaspoons sea salt. Set aside.

For the caramel shapes and shards, gently heat the sugar in a pan until melted and golden. Shake the pan towards the end to allow any unmelted sugar to melt. Spoon half the caramel onto the greased baking sheet, then drag it outwards with the back of the spoon to create a rough square shape with one thinner, uneven side. Sprinkle the cake sprinkle mixture over part of the rectangle. Use the spoon to drizzle the remaining caramel into spiral shapes and zig-zag patterns. Leave to harden. Break the square shape into shards.

When ready to serve, push the caramel shapes into the top of the cake, drizzle with the caramel sauce and decorate with the blackberries and lemon thyme sprigs. Spray with the edible gold spray (if using).

Cook's tip:
You'll have some caramel sauce left over; it's great served with the cake for those wanting an extra drizzle! It's so delicious you'll want to pour it over every cake and dessert – keep any remaining sauce in the fridge, covered, for up to 1 week or allow to cool for 5 minutes, reserve what you need for the cake and ladle the remaining sauce into a sterilized jar. Seal and allow to cool. It will keep for up to 3 months.

Vegan tip:
Always check ingredients on individual products to ensure they are suitable for a vegan diet. Different brands may vary.

Eastern promise

After putting back that Oriental-style floral black and gold satin bomber jacket in favour of a more practical Hunter rain jacket, I couldn't forget that sumptuous colour combo and silky texture – so here's an edible version to dive into after getting caught in the rain!

50 g/2 oz. gold flower modelling paste

1 tablespoon runny honey

1 teaspoon white sugar pearls

1 quantity of Double Chocolate Sponge mixture (see page 16) baked in three greased and lined 18-cm/7-inch cake pans for 40 minutes until an inserted cocktail stick/toothpick comes out clean, then cooled

¼ quantity of Classic Buttercream (see page 20)

1 quantity of Glossy Black Fudge Icing (see page 23)

8–10 edible clear gems (optional)

set of 4 flower plunger cutters

small piece of foam (a new foam scouring pad is ideal)

small ball cake tool

baking sheet lined with baking parchment

small paintbrush

leaf plunger cutter

disposable piping/pastry bag

SERVES 20

To make the flowers and leaves, knead the gold modelling paste until soft. Roll out between two sheets of baking parchment to as thin as possible. Using the flower plunger cutters, stamp out 28 flowers – seven large, seven medium, seven small and seven very small. To curl the petals, place a flower on a small piece of foam and, using the small ball cake tool, gently press the centre. Put the flower on the lined baking sheet, then continue to 'curl' about half of the flowers. Leave the remaining half flat. Brush the centres of some of the flowers with honey and stick on a sugar pearl. Stamp out 3–4 leaf shapes using the leaf cutter, bend slightly and set aside with the flowers to dry overnight.

If necessary, trim the tops of the cakes to make level. Sandwich together using the buttercream – the bottom side of the top cake should be facing up. Place the cake on a serving plate or cake board.

Reserve 200 g/7 oz. of the glossy black fudge icing, then crumb-coat (see page 11) the cake in a thin layer using some of the remaining icing. Smooth and remove the excess with a palette knife/metal spatula. Chill in the fridge for 15 minutes. Use the remaining icing to coat the cake in a thick second layer. Smooth and remove the excess icing with a palette knife/metal spatula.

Fill the piping/pastry bag with the reserved icing. Snip a 2.5-cm/1-inch hole at the tip of the bag and pipe small blobs around the top of the cake. Gently press the gold flowers and leaves onto the side and top of the cake. Brush the centres of some of the remaining undecorated flowers with a little honey and use to stick on an edible clear gem (if using).

Dark angel

For those creative little angels with a cheeky naughty streak!

¼ quantity of Classic Buttercream (see page 20)

purple gel or paste food colouring

1 quantity of Double Chocolate Sponge mixture (see page 16) baked in three greased and lined 18-cm/7-inch cake pans for 40 minutes until an inserted cocktail stick/ toothpick comes out clean, then cooled

½ quantity of Glossy Black Fudge Icing (see page 23)

2 tablespoons each purple chocolate flake sprinkles and sugar crystal sprinkles

100 g/3½ oz. dark/bittersweet chocolate, broken into pieces

edible silver spray

1 quantity of Royal Icing (see page 22)

disposable piping/pastry bag fitted with a small round nozzle/tip

disposable piping/pastry bag fitted with a 2d Wilton nozzle/ tip (or a medium curved 6 pointed star nozzle/tip)

SERVES 20

Mix the buttercream with a little of the purple food colouring to get a light-mid shade. If necessary, trim the tops of the cakes to make level. Sandwich together using the coloured buttercream – the bottom side of the top cake should be facing up. Place the cake on a cake board or plate.

Reserve 200 g/7 oz. of the glossy black fudge icing. Crumb-coat (see page 11) the cake in a thin layer using some of the remaining icing. Place in the fridge to chill for 15 minutes. Then use the remaining icing to coat the cake in a thick second layer. Smooth and remove the excess icing with a palette knife/metal spatula. Gently press the sprinkles onto the base section of the icing. Chill for 1 hour.

Draw the outlines of two 'wings' onto a piece of parchment paper, start with a right-angled triangle, 10 cm/4 inches along the base and 10 cm/4 inches along the vertical straight side. Join the 'end points' together with a slight wave to complete the triangle shape. Turn over and place on a baking sheet.

Melt the dark/bittersweet chocolate in a heatproof bowl set over a pan of simmering water (or microwave on high in 30-second bursts, stirring in between). Fill the piping/pastry bag fitted with the small round nozzle/tip with most of the melted chocolate. Pipe around each wing shape and then swirl the chocolate in small spirals until the middle is filled (pipe along sections of the outline twice if the chocolate looks thin). Freeze until needed, then spray with edible silver spray.

Place another piece of parchment paper on a baking sheet, spoon on the remaining chocolate and spread it into an approximate 10 x 12-cm/ 4 x 5-inch rectangle. Place in the freezer until needed, then break into small shards and spray with edible silver spray.

Add enough purple colouring to the royal icing to get a deep shade, and add a little water, if needed, to achieve a thick, but pourable consistency. Pour some around the top edge of the cake, allowing it to drip down the sides, then pour the rest over the top of the cake and smooth with a palette knife/metal spatula. Leave to set for 4 hours or overnight.

When the icing has thickened but not completely set with a fine crust, fill the piping/pastry bag fitted with the 2d Wilton nozzle/tip with the reserved black icing. Carefully pipe 3–4 rose shapes on top of the cake, swirling from the inside-out, then decorate with the silver chocolate 'wings' and shards. Spray the top of the cake with a little more edible silver spray, if liked.

Frills and spills

1.95 kg/4 lb. 5 oz. Classic Buttercream (see page 20, with quantities: 375 g/3½ sticks minus 1½ tablespoons unsalted butter, 275 g/9½ oz. vegetable fat, 1.3 kg/9¼ cups icing/confectioners' sugar and 2–3 tablespoons water)

turquoise gel or paste food colouring

1 quantity of Traditional Vanilla Sponge mixture (see page 14) baked in three greased and lined 18-cm/7-inch cake pans for 35–40 minutes until an inserted cocktail stick/toothpick comes out clean, then cooled

60 g/2¼ oz. large white sugar pearls

10 small sugar pearls

175 g/6 oz. white chocolate

iridescent lustre (optional)

2 small disposable piping/pastry bags

large disposable piping/pastry bag fitted with a 125 Wilton petal nozzle/tip

SERVES 20

Reserve 275 g/9½ oz. of the buttercream and stir through enough turquoise colouring to get a very pale shade. Set aside.

If necessary, trim the tops of the cakes to make level. Sandwich together using 350 g/12 oz. of the remaining buttercream – the bottom side of the top cake should be facing up. Place on a serving plate. Crumb-coat (see page 11) the cake using 400 g/14 oz. of the buttercream. Chill for 15 minutes.

Colour the remaining buttercream a light-mid shade of turquoise. Set aside 275 g/9½ oz. of this colour and use the remainder to coat the cake in a second layer. Smooth with a palette knife/metal spatula.

Fill a small piping/pastry bag with 100 g/3½ oz. of the reserved very pale turquoise buttercream and fill another small piping/pastry bag with 100 g/3½ oz. of the reserved light-mid turquoise buttercream. Snip a 1-cm//³⁄₈-inch hole in the end of each. Place the filled smaller bags inside the large piping/pastry bag fitted with the petal nozzle/tip. Use the 'base' from a loose-bottomed cake pan as the surface onto which to pipe your flower. Pipe little clusters of waves so they butt up against each other and even overlap a bit – you don't need to be too neat, just build it up and keep your piping contained to a 12-cm/4³⁄₄-inch circle. Place in the freezer to harden.

Re-fill the small piping/pastry bags with the remaining 175 g/6 oz. of the very pale turquoise buttercream and the darker buttercream. Place inside the larger bag again, fitted with the petal nozzle/tip. Carefully pipe around the cake from the bottom; gently squeeze the buttercream from the bag holding the tip next to the cake with the rounded end at the top and the point at the bottom. Move it in gentle undulating motions as you work around the cake to get a light ruffled effect, covering about one-third of the side of the cake. Use the sugar pearls to decorate above the frills.

Melt the chocolate in a heatproof bowl set over a pan of simmering water (or microwave on high in 30-second bursts, stirring in between). Remove the cake from the fridge. Pour the melted chocolate around the edge of the top of the cake, allowing it to trickle down the sides. Continue drizzling in a spiral motion, moving inwards to cover the top of the cake. Gently sweep a long palette knife/metal spatula across the top to smooth the chocolate. Let set.

Once set, use a fish slice to transfer the hardened buttercream flower to the cake. Brush the chocolate with iridescent lustre, if liked. Allow the buttercream flower to soften before serving. Use a warmed knife to cut.

Pink fizz cake

strawberry extract or flavouring (check the brand as to how much you need – there is approx.1.65 kg/3 lb. 10 oz. of sponge mixture)

1 quantity of Traditional Vanilla Sponge mixture (see page 14)

pink paste or gel food colouring

1.2 kg/2 lb. 10 oz. Classic Buttercream (see page 20, with quantities: 250 g/ 2¼ sticks unsalted butter, 150 g/5 oz. vegetable fat, 800 g/5¾ cups icing/ confectioners' sugar and 2–3 tablespoons water)

For the pink fizz jellies

6 leaves gelatine

1 bottle prosecco (750 ml/3 cups)

4 tablespoons caster/ superfine sugar

For the rhubarb ribbon

300 g/10½ oz. rhubarb

For the pink fizz bark

200 g/7 oz. white chocolate, broken into pieces

340 g/12 oz. pink Candy Melts

1 teaspoon popping candy

1 tablespoon pink shimmer crunch

2 teaspoons pink sugar crystals

8 100-ml/3½-fl. oz. plastic disposable champagne flutes with removable bases

2 20-cm/8-inch cake pans, greased and lined

4 baking sheets lined with baking parchment

SERVES 24

One for the Pink Lady in all of us...

For the pink fizz jellies, place the gelatine in cold water to soak. Heat 250 ml/ 1 cup of the prosecco with the sugar until almost boiling. Squeeze the excess water from the gelatine, add to the pan and stir until dissolved. Return to a very gentle heat if it needs assistance in melting fully. Top up with the remaining prosecco. Divide between the disposable champagne flutes. Transfer to the fridge for 4 hours to set, leaning a couple at a slight angle. You will only need three jellies for the cake, the rest can be served alongside.

Preheat the oven to 180°C (350°F) Gas 4. Stir the strawberry extract through the sponge mix and colour it a mid-pink shade. Divide between the cake pans. Bake for 45–50 minutes until an inserted cocktail stick/toothpick comes out clean. Cool in the pans for 10 minutes, then turn out onto a wire rack.

For the rhubarb ribbon, reduce the oven to 110°C (225°F) Gas ¼. Using a vegetable peeler, peel off the pink outer layer of the rhubarb. Place in swirly patterns on a lined baking sheet and twist around the handles of wooden spoons, if liked. Bake for 20–30 minutes until dried out. Set aside to cool.

For the bark, melt the white chocolate and the pink Candy Melts in two separate heatproof bowls set over pans of simmering water (or microwave each on high in 30 second bursts, stirring in between). Place the three remaining lined baking sheets in 'landscape' position in front of you. The aim is to get three 12 x 28-cm/5 x 11-inch rectangles of chocolate made up of the two colours. Spoon one-third of the melted pink Candy Melts onto one baking sheet, spread out to a thin strip, 6 x 28 cm/2½ x 11 inches. Spoon one-third of the white chocolate above it so the colours touch, then smooth out to complete the 12 x 28-cm/5 x 11-inch rectangle. Swirl the colours where they meet with a cocktail stick/toothpick. Scatter over the popping candy, shimmer crunch and sugar crystals. Repeat twice more with the remaining chocolate and baking sheets. Freeze for 20 minutes, then gently roll up the baking parchment, allowing the bark to snap into shards. Chill until needed.

Colour the buttercream a mid-pink shade. If necessary, trim the tops of the cakes to make level. Sandwich together using 250 g/9 oz. of the buttercream – the bottom side of the top cake should be facing up. Place on a plate. Crumb-coat (see page 11) the cake using 450 g/1 lb. of the buttercream. Place in the fridge for 15 minutes, then use the remaining buttercream to coat the cake in a second layer. Smooth with a palette knife/metal spatula.

Gently press the bark into the sides of the cake to cover. Remove the bases from the 'angled' filled champagne flutes and use to decorate the top with one more flute and the rhubarb ribbons. Serve with the remaining jellies.

All that shimmers

The perfect cake for a 50th wedding anniversary. Relax and enjoy painting this sparkly little number – it's my equivalent to an adult colouring book... with the added bonus – it's edible!

1 quantity of Traditional Vanilla Sponge mixture (see page 14) baked in three greased and lined 18-cm/7-inch cake pans for 35–40 minutes until an inserted cocktail stick/toothpick comes out clean, then cooled

1 quantity of Classic Buttercream (see page 20)

200 g/7 oz. yellow fondant icing

edible piping gel

60 g/2¼ oz. edible confetti

200 g/7 oz. white chocolate, broken into pieces

edible gold paint

edible gold lustre (optional)

For the decoration

60 g/2¼ oz. white flower modelling paste

2 tablespoons icing/confectioners' sugar

edible gold spray

'50' sign (optional)

6 champagne truffles

20 g/¾ oz. white chocolate, melted

baking sheet lined with baking parchment

soft-bristled paintbrush

SERVES 20

To prepare the decoration, roll the white modelling paste into four narrow 23-cm/9-inch sausage shapes, tapering the ends into points. Place on the lined baking sheet and bend the tops round into spiral shapes. Put into two pairs so the spiralled tops on each pair form the top of a heart shape. Allow the ends to touch lightly, then slightly curve round. Let harden for 2 hours.

To 'glue' the halves together, mix the icing/confectioners' sugar with a few drops of water to form a thick paste. With the hearts still in position on the baking sheet, paint a little paste in the places where curves meet. Press together gently and leave overnight to dry fully. Once dry, spray the surface of the hearts with the edible gold spray.

If necessary, trim the tops of the cakes to make level. Sandwich together using 350 g/12 oz. of the buttercream – the bottom side of the top cake should be facing up. Place the cake on a plate. Crumb-coat (see page 11) the cake using 450 g/1 lb. of the buttercream. Chill for 15 minutes, then use the remaining buttercream to coat the cake in a second layer. Smooth and remove the excess buttercream with a palette knife/metal spatula.

Roll out the yellow fondant icing to a thin strip approximately 7 x 60 cm/3 x 24 inches and wrap around the base of the cake. Trim so the ends are butting up against each other rather than overlapping.

Brush the fondant with piping gel and gently press on the confetti, re-gathering the 'dropped' confetti every so often, until the fondant is covered – a few small gaps are fine. Leave for a couple of hours to set.

Melt the white chocolate in a heatproof bowl set over a pan of simmering water (or microwave on high in 30-second bursts, stirring in between). Remove the cake from the fridge. Pour the melted chocolate around the edge of the top of the cake, allowing it to trickle down the sides. Continue drizzling the chocolate in a spiral motion moving inwards to cover the top of the cake. Gently sweep a palette knife/metal spatula across the top and insert the '50' sign (if using). Allow to set.

Brush the drips and confetti with 2–3 coats of edible gold paint, allowing it to dry fully between coats. Brush the gold with gold lustre dust, if liked. Position the champagne truffles and secure in place using the 20 g/¾ oz. of melted white chocolate. Once set, use them to lean the gold hearts against.

Fancy fondant fancies

There is nothing better than a homemade gift. These elegant fondant fancies make a great Mother's Day present or are the perfect way to finish off a decadent birthday tea.

90 g/3¼ oz. white flower modelling paste

yellow gel or paste food colouring

runny honey, for brushing

½ quantity Traditional Vanilla Sponge mixture (see page 14) baked in a 20-cm/8-inch square loose-bottomed cake pan for 35–40 minutes, until an inserted cocktail stick/toothpick comes out clean, then cooled

250 g/2¼ sticks butter, softened

250 g/1¾ cups icing/confectioners' sugar, sifted

3 tablespoons smooth apricot jam/jelly

200 g/7 oz. marzipan

750 g/1 lb. 10 oz. orange fondant icing, cubed

orange blossom water (optional)

large daisy-shaped flower plunger cutter

small piece of foam (a new foam scouring pad is ideal)

small ball cake tool

baking sheet lined with baking parchment

disposable piping/pastry bag

petit four cases (optional)

MAKES 25

Knead the flower modelling paste until soft. Colour 10 g/⅓ oz. yellow and wrap in clingfilm/plastic wrap until needed. Roll the rest of the modelling paste between two sheets of baking parchment as thinly as possible. Using the large daisy-shaped flower plunger cutter, stamp out 25 flowers.

To curl the petals, place a flower on a small piece of foam and, using the small ball cake tool, gently press the centre. Put the flower on the baking sheet lined with baking parchment and 'curl' the remaining flowers. Roll the yellow modelling paste into 25 small balls. Brush the centres of the flowers with a little honey and use to stick on the small balls of yellow modelling paste. Set aside to dry overnight.

Place the cake in the freezer to chill for 10 minutes. Meanwhile make the buttercream. Beat the butter until smooth and pale, then gradually add the icing/confectioners' sugar and beat until smooth. Cover and set aside.

For the marzipan topping, heat the apricot jam/jelly in a small pan and mix well to loosen. Remove from the heat, stir again, then brush the top of the cake with the jam/jelly. Roll out the marzipan as thinly as possible and use to cover the top of the cake. Place the cake in the freezer for 10 minutes.

Trim the top and sides of the cake to create a perfect square, then cut into 25 equal squares. With a dinner knife, cover four sides of each square with buttercream (not the marzipan top or the base). Put the remaining buttercream in the piping/pastry bag and snip off the tip. Pipe a blob of buttercream in the centre of each square on top of the marzipan. Dab the top with a wet finger to flatten the peak. Place in the freezer for 10 minutes to chill again.

For the icing, beat the fondant icing in a free-standing mixer with a paddle attachment (or whisk in a bowl using an electric hand whisk fitted with dough hooks) until softened, adding a tablespoon of water if it's too hard. Very gradually add 150 ml/⅔ cup water – the icing will become smooth and more liquid. The consistency should coat the back of a spoon; add more water, if necessary. Add a few drops of orange blossom water to taste, if using.

Insert a fork into each cake, one at a time, at a slight angle. Spoon over the icing to coat, then carefully set onto a wire rack. Position a flower on top of each and leave to set. Once set, place in petit four cases, if liked.

Winter crystals

This geode effect cake is traditionally made with rock candy which is much easier to get hold of in America, or you can 'grow your own'. For a simple but striking cheat, this version uses crushed hard-boiled sweets/hard candies.

325 g/scant 3 sticks butter

650 g/4²/₃ cups icing/confectioners' sugar, plus extra for dusting

1 quantity of Traditional Vanilla Sponge Cake mixture (see page 14) baked in three 18-cm/7-inch cake pans for 35–40 minutes until an inserted cocktail stick/toothpick comes out clean, then cooled

1 kg/2 lb. 4 oz. white fondant icing

60 g/2¹/₄ oz. grey fondant icing

85 g/3 oz. white opaque hard-boiled sweets/hard candies

85 g/3 oz. pink (or colour of your choice) hard-boiled sweets/hard candies

75 g/2¹/₂ oz. edible piping gel

edible gold leaf

2 small paintbrushes

SERVES 20

To make the buttercream base for the fondant, beat the butter with an electric hand whisk until pale and creamy, then gradually beat in the icing/confectioners' sugar with 1 tablespoon of water until smooth and creamy. Add another 1 tablespoon of water, if necessary.

If necessary, trim the tops of the cakes to make level. Set aside 150 g/5 oz. of the buttercream. Sandwich together using 350 g/12 oz. of the buttercream – the bottom side of the top cake should be facing up. Crumb-coat (see page 11) the cake using the remaining buttercream.

Dust the surface with icing/confectioners' sugar and knead the white fondant, then roll out to an approximate 20-cm/8-inch circle. Knead the grey fondant and roll into sausage shapes of differing sizes. Press into the top of the white fondant, then knead briefly until marbled. Roll out the fondant to a circle large enough to cover the cake, about 47 cm/19 inches in diameter.

Use a rolling pin to help lift the fondant over the cake and gently press around the top edge of the cake with your hands to stick the fondant to the cake. Gently 'flair out' the icing as you work downwards, lightly pressing the fondant against the cake. Smooth with cake smoothers or the palms of your hands. Trim the bottom edge with a sharp knife. Transfer the cake to a plate.

With a long, sharp knife, cut a jagged wedge out of the top and side of the front of the cake, approximately 7 cm/2³/₄ inches wide – try not to cut too far into the cake as you will find it difficult to stick the sugar crystals in. Cut a slightly smaller wedge out of the top and side at the back of the cake. Coat the exposed cake with the reserved buttercream; apply blobs of buttercream using the tip of a dinner knife until completely covered, then smooth over.

To make the sugar crystals, keeping the two colours separate, use a pestle and mortar to crush the hard-boiled sweets/hard candies into both small and chunky pieces. Working on the front recess first, using a paintbrush, paint a thick layer of the piping gel over the buttercream and stick the pink sugar crystals into the centre. Stick a combination of the pink and opaque crystals around it, then finish with an outer edge of opaque sugar crystals. Repeat on the recess at the back. Dust the crystals with a little icing/confectioners' sugar. Keeping the gold leaf between the paper sheets, cut the sheets into strips. Brush the fondant at the edge of the recesses with a little water, then use the second paintbrush to attach gold leaf to the cake.

Club tropicana mug cake

No jet lag here. Get a taste of sunshine in 3 minutes with this lusciously tropical, fruity mug cake.

5 tablespoons self-raising/
 self-rising flour

4 tablespoons caster/
 superfine sugar

3 tablespoons vegetable oil

3 tablespoons coconut milk

1 egg, beaten

½ passion fruit, pulp and seeds

2 tablespoons finely chopped
 ripe mango flesh

**For the topping and
 decoration**

squirty cream

1 cocktail cherry

orange slice

lime slice and grated zest

cocktail umbrella (optional)

SERVES 1

Place all the cake ingredients in a large mug (approx. 250 ml/1 cup). Mix well with a fork. Microwave at 800W for 3 minutes until cooked through.

Serve with a spiral of squirty cream. Decorate with the cocktail cherry, slice of orange, slice of lime and grated zest. Top with the cocktail umbrella, if using.

Flamingo cake

1 quantity of Traditional Vanilla Sponge mixture (see page 14) baked in three greased and lined 18-cm/7-inch cake pans for 35–40 minutes until an inserted cocktail stick/toothpick comes out clean, then cooled

1.75 kg/3 lb 14 oz. of Classic Buttercream (see page 20, with quantities: 350 g/3 sticks unsalted butter, 250 g/1¼ cups vegetable fat and 1.15 kg/8 cups icing/confectioners' sugar)

pink gel or paste food colouring

150 g/5 oz. mixture of pink and white sprinkles, such as pink and white pearls, dried raspberry pieces, dark and light pink sprinkle sugar

For the pond

75 g/6 tablespoons caster/superfine sugar

1 tablespoon cornflour/cornstarch

4 tablespoons lemon juice

blue gel or paste food colouring

cocktail stick/toothpick

3 small disposable piping/pastry bags

1 small star nozzle/tip

60 cm/2 feet white and pink striped ribbon

1 Wilton 366 leaf nozzle/tip

large disposable piping/pastry bag

2 model flamingos

small plastic greenery – try your local pet shop, you can get the most amazing green stuff for fish tanks!

SERVES 20

For the 'pond', place all the ingredients except the colouring in a pan with 4 tablespoons of water. Bring to the boil, stirring occasionally, then allow to cool. Stir through a smear of blue colouring from the end of a cocktail stick/toothpick. Cover and set aside.

If necessary, trim the tops of the cakes to make level. Sandwich together using 350 g/12 oz. of the buttercream – the bottom side of the top cake should be facing up. Place the cake on a serving plate or cake board. Add a little pink colouring to the rest of the buttercream to get a light pastel shade. Crumb-coat (see page 11) the cake using 400 g/14 oz. of the buttercream. Place in the fridge for 15 minutes, then use 550 g/19 oz. of the remaining buttercream to coat the cake in a second layer. Smooth and remove the excess buttercream with a palette knife/metal spatula. Put the excess buttercream back into the bowl.

Divide the remaining buttercream between two bowls, leave the first bowl the light pastel shade, then add a little more colouring to the second bowl to get a darker shade. Cover the bowls with clingfilm/plastic wrap and set aside.

Mask off the bottom half of the cake by wrapping round a piece of baking parchment approximately 8 x 60 cm/3 inches x 2 feet long, gently pressing into place. Cut out a kidney shape from baking parchment to mask off the 'pond' and gently press on the top of the cake. Place the cake in a large baking pan to catch the sprinkles. Mix all the sprinkles together in a bowl and gently press the sprinkles onto the exposed buttercream, regathering as necessary.

Remove the baking parchment. To finish the edges of the 'pond', mix 2 tablespoons of each of the pink buttercreams together and use to fill a small piping/pastry bag fitted with the small star nozzle/tip, pipe little star shapes next to each other to outline the 'pond' (ensure they are touching). Wrap the pink and white striped ribbon round the base of the cake.

Place the Wilton 366 leaf nozzle/tip inside the large piping/pastry bag. Fill one of the remaining small disposable piping/pastry bags with the pale pink buttercream and the other with the dark pink buttercream. Snip approximately 1 cm/³/₈ inch from the end of each. Place both in the large piping/pastry bag with the leaf nozzle/tip and twist the end. Working just above the ribbon, squeeze the two-tone buttercream from the piping/pastry bag in 1.5-cm/½-inch downwards motions. Work all around the cake, then complete two more layers until the piped buttercream meets the sprinkles.

Spoon the blue 'pond water' into the recess on the top of the cake. Decorate with the model flamingos and plastic plants.

Index

A

After Eight mini cakes 83
all that shimmers 146
almonds: croccante 91
   pineapple passion 29
apple and pear crisp 53
apricot jam: fancy fondant fancies 149
arctic tower cake, raspberry ripple 37
avocado frosting 54
avocado love 34

B

baby shower cake 65
bags, piping/pastry 8
baking parchment 8
   lining pans 11
bananas: vegan chocolate sponge 19
bark: glam rock bark 125
   pink fizz bark 145
   popcorn bag bark 114
   unicorn bark 100
   wild birch bark 58
batters: dessert-style sponge 18
   double chocolate sponge 16
   gluten-free double chocolate sponge 16
   gluten-free vanilla sponge 15
   traditional vanilla sponge 14
   vegan chocolate sponge 19
biscuits/cookies: blueberry blues 26
   bonfire night bonanza 50
   boy or girl baby shower cake 65
   couture stiletto cupcakes 132
   fright night cake 54
   high drama 122
   rocky road muffins 76
   seaside breeze 121
black fudge icing 23
blackberries: Britalian trifle layer cake 91
   fallen fruit chocolate cake 53
   sultry salted caramel 137
blueberries: blueberry blues 26
   Britalian trifle layer cake 91
bonfire night bonanza 50
bouquet, cake pop 46
bow, flower modelling paste 92
boy or girl baby shower cake 65
brilliant white buttercream 21
Britalian trifle layer cake 91

bunting 117
buttercream 12
   brilliant white buttercream 21
   classic buttercream 20
   crumb-coating 11
   lemon buttercream 33
   two-ingredient buttercream 20
butterfly ball cake 126
buttermilk: glossy black fudge icing 23

C

cake batters see batters
cake pans 8
   lining 11
cake pop bouquet 46
candies see sweets
candy floss/cotton candy:
   fairground fun cake 117
candy melts: cake pop bouquet 46
   ice queen frozen cake 61
   lightning strikes 125
   melting ice-cream drippy cakes 88
   pink fizz bark 145
   popcorn bag bark 114
   unicorn bark 100
candy shop show-stopper 72
caramel: croccante 91
   film lover cake 114
   sultry salted caramel 137
champagne truffles: all that shimmers 146
cheesecake: blueberry blues 26
chocolate: After Eight mini cakes 83
   all that shimmers 146
   bonfire night bonanza 50
   boy or girl baby shower cake 65
   Britalian trifle layer cake 91
   cake pop bouquet 46
   couture stiletto cupcakes 132
   dark angel 141
   dazzling mallow teacake 'cakes' 87
   double chocolate sponge 16
   drizzling chocolate 12
   dunkin donuts cake 80
   Easter egg cake 62
   Eastern promise 138
   fallen fruit chocolate cake 53
   Ferrero Rocher cake 79
   fig and pistachio cupcakes 38
   fright night cake 54
   frills and spills 142
   ganache 62, 76, 83
   giant jaffa cake 75

glam rock cake 125
glaze 107
glossy black fudge icing 23
gluten-free double chocolate sponge 16
high drama 122
hugs and meringue kisses 108
ice queen frozen cake 61
melting ice-cream drippy cakes 88
meringue mushrooms 99
nests 62
pineapple passion 29
pink fizz bark 145
popcorn bag bark 114
red velvet crepe cake 84
rocky road muffins 76
seaside breeze 121
speech bubbles 130
sprinkle spectacular cake 92
sunflower cake 42
triple chocolate drip cake 66
unicorn dreamer 100
vegan chocolate sponge 19
watercolour washout 118
watermelon wonder 30
white chocolate shards 37
wild birch Christmas cake 58
see also Nutella
Christmas bakes: Christmas shimmer baubles 57
   wild birch Christmas cake 58
citrus sensation 33
classic buttercream 20
club tropicana mug cake 153
cocktail sticks 8
coconut: fairground fun cake 117
coconut milk: club tropicana mug cake 153
   vegan salted caramel sauce 137
cookies see biscuits
cotton candy see candy floss
couture stiletto cupcakes 132
cream: Britalian trifle layer cake 91
   Ferrero Rocher cake 79
   ganache 62, 76, 83
   triple chocolate drip cake 66
   Wimbledon tennis towers 129
cream cheese: red velvet crepe cake 84
crepe cake, red velvet 84
crisps, apple and pear 53
croccante 91
crumb-coating 11
cupcakes: couture stiletto 132
   fig and pistachio 38

D
dark angel 141
dazzling mallow teacake 'cakes' 87
decorations: flowers 34
  glam rock bark 125
  lightning strikes 125
  pink fizz bark 145
  piping roses 41
  popcorn bag bark 114
  speech bubbles 130
  unicorn bark 100
  white chocolate shards 37
  white chocolate snowflakes 61
  wild birch bark 58
dessert-style sponge 18
digestive biscuits/graham crackers:
blueberry blues 26
  rocky road muffins 76
  seaside breeze 121
dinner knives 8
disposable piping/pastry bags 8
double chocolate sponge 16
doughnuts: dunkin donuts cake 80
drizzling: chocolate 12
  fruit sauces 12
  icing 12
dunkin donuts cake 80

E F
Easter egg cake 62
Eastern promise 138
equipment 8
fairground fun cake 117
fallen fruit chocolate cake 53
fancy fondant fancies 149
Ferrero Rocher cake 79
figs: fig and pistachio cupcakes 38
  fallen fruit chocolate cake 53
film lover cake 114
final coat, icing 11
finishing touches 11–12
fireworks, bonfire night bonanza 50
flamingo cake 154
flowers: butterfly ball cake 126
  couture stiletto cupcakes 132
  decorating cakes with 34
  Hello petal! 45
  ombre two-tier rose cake 41
  sunflower cake 42
  ultra violet 103
fondant fancies 149
food processors, making
  buttercream 12
fright night cake 54
frills and spills 142
frostings and icings: avocado

frosting 54
brilliant white buttercream 21
classic buttercream 20
cover-ups 11
crumb-coating 11
drizzling 12
final coat 11
ganache 62
glaze 107
glossy black fudge icing 23
lemon buttercream 33
royal icing 22
two-ingredient buttercream 20
fruit: drizzling fruit sauces 12
  fallen fruit chocolate cake 53
  fright night cake 54
  see also apples, raspberries etc
fudge icing, glossy black 23

G
ganache 62, 76, 83
gelatine: glaze 107
  pink fizz jellies 145
giant jaffa cake 75
glacé icing, drizzling 12
glam rock cake 125
glaze 107
glossy black fudge icing 23
glucose: glaze 107
gluten-free double chocolate
  sponge 16
gluten-free vanilla sponge 15
graham crackers see digestive
  biscuits

H
Halloween: fright night cake 54
hard-boiled sweets/hard candies:
  After Eight mini cakes 83
  bonfire night bonanza 50
  ice queen frozen cake 61
  mermaid cake 111
  winter crystals 150
hazelnuts: Ferrero Rocher cake 79
Hello petal! 45
high drama 122
honey: Eastern promise 138
  fig and pistachio cupcakes 38
  watercolour washout 118
hugs and meringue kisses 108

I
ice cream: raspberry ripple arctic
  tower cake 37
ice-cream cones: Mad Hatters tea
  party cake 99

melting ice-cream drippy cakes
  88
mermaid cake 111
seaside breeze 121
unicorn dreamer 100
ice queen frozen cake 61
icing see frostings

J K L
jaffa cake, giant 75
jam/jelly: Britalian trifle layer cake 91
  fancy fondant fancies 149
jellies, pink fizz 145
knives 8
lemon: buttercream 33
  citrus sensation 33
lightning strikes 125
lining pans 11
liquorice/licorice: film lover cake 114
  glam rock cake 125
lolly pops: fairground fun cake 117

M
M&Ms: boy or girl baby shower
  cake 65
  high drama 122
macarons: butterfly ball cake 126
Mad Hatters tea party cake 99
mangoes: club tropicana mug cake
  153
maple syrup: vegan chocolate
  sponge 19
marmalade: giant jaffa cake 75
marshmallows: bonfire night
  bonanza 50
  dazzling mallow teacake 'cakes' 87
  rocky road muffins 76
  Seventies swirl cake 96
marzipan: fancy fondant fancies 149
mascarpone: blueberry blues 26
  Britalian trifle layer cake 91
  fig and pistachio cupcakes 38
melting ice-cream drippy cakes 88
meringue: hugs and meringue
  kisses 108
  meringue kisses 100
  meringue mushrooms 99
mermaid cake 111
metal spatulas 8
milk, adding to buttercream 12
mint: After Eight mini cakes 83
  cake pop bouquet 46
  Wimbledon tennis towers 129
modern art mirror cake 107
muffins, rocky road 76
mushrooms, meringue 99

N O

nests, Easter egg cake 62
nozzles/tips, piping 8
Nutella: Ferrero Rocher cake 79
　fig and pistachio cupcakes 38
　sunflower cake 42
ombre two-tier rose cake 41
orange jelly/jello: giant jaffa cake 75
Oreo cookies: boy or girl baby
　shower cake 65
　high drama 122

P

palette knives 8
pancakes: red velvet crepe cake 84
pans 8
　lining 11
Parma violets: ultra violet 103
passion fruit: club tropicana mug
　cake 153
peanut butter cups: film lover cake
　114
pears: apple and pear crisp 53
physalis: fallen fruit chocolate cake
　53
Pimm's: Wimbledon tennis towers
　129
pinata cake 69
pineapple passion 29
pink fizz cake 145
piping nozzles/tips 8
piping/pastry bags 8
piping roses 41
pistachio nuts: avocado love 34
　fig and pistachio cupcakes 38
popcorn: film lover cake 114
popping candy: pink fizz bark 145
pretzels: film lover cake 114
prosecco: pink fizz jellies 145

R

rainbow drops cake 104
raspberries: avocado love 34
　Britalian trifle layer cake 91
　raspberry ripple arctic tower cake
　37
raspberry jam/jelly: Britalian trifle
　layer cake 91
red velvet crepe cake 84
rhubarb ribbon 145
rice vermicelli: nests 62
rocky road muffins 76
roses: avocado love 34
　butterfly ball cake 126
　couture stiletto cupcakes 132

ombre two-tier rose cake 41
royal icing 22
　drizzling 12

S

salt: sultry salted caramel 137
satsumas: Wimbledon tennis towers
　129
sauces: raspberry sauce 37
　vegan salted caramel sauce 137
seaside breeze 121
Seventies swirl cake 96
sherry: Britalian trifle layer cake 91
shower cake 65
skewers, wooden 8
small cakes: After Eight mini cakes
　83
　cake pop bouquet 46
　Christmas shimmer baubles 57
　couture stiletto cupcakes 132
　dazzling mallow teacake 'cakes'
　87
　fancy fondant fancies 149
　fig and pistachio cupcakes 38
　rocky road muffins 76
　Wimbledon tennis towers 129
Smarties: boy or girl baby shower
　cake 65
snowflakes, white chocolate 61
soured/sour cream: red velvet crepe
　cake 84
soya milk: vegan chocolate sponge
　19
spatulas 8
speech bubble decorations 130
sponges: dessert-style sponge 18
　double chocolate sponge 16
　gluten-free double chocolate
　　sponge 16
　gluten-free vanilla sponge 15
　traditional vanilla sponge 14
　vegan chocolate sponge 19
stiletto cupcakes 132
strawberries: Britalian trifle layer
　cake 91
　Wimbledon tennis towers 129
sultry salted caramel 137
sunflower cake 42
super hero cake 130
sweets: After Eight mini cakes 83
　bonfire night bonanza 50
　candy shop show-stopper 72
　ice queen frozen cake 61
　mermaid cake 111
　pinata cake 69
　winter crystals 150

T

teacake 'cakes', dazzling mallow 87
techniques 11–12
tennis towers 129
toffee popcorn: film lover cake 114
toothpicks 8
traditional vanilla sponge 14
trifle layer cake, Britalian 91
triple chocolate drip cake 66
truffles: all that shimmers 146
two-ingredient buttercream 20

U V

ultra violet 103
unicorn dreamer 100
vanilla: gluten-free vanilla sponge 15
　red velvet crepe cake 84
　traditional vanilla sponge 14
vegan recipes: brilliant white
　buttercream 21
　vegan chocolate sponge 19
　vegan salted caramel sauce 137
vermicelli: nests 62
violets: ultra violet 103

W

walnuts: fallen fruit chocolate cake
　53
water, adding to buttercream 12
watercolour washout 118
watermelon wonder 30
whisks, making buttercream 12
white chocolate: After Eight mini
　cakes 83
　all that shimmers 146
　cake pop bouquet 46
　couture stiletto cupcakes 132
　Easter egg cake 62
　frills and spills 142
　glaze 107
　ice queen frozen cake 61
　melting ice-cream drippy cakes 88
　pink fizz bark 145
　popcorn bag bark 114
　seaside breeze 121
　triple chocolate drip cake 66
　unicorn bark 100
　unicorn dreamer 100
　watercolour washout 118
　white chocolate shards 37
　white chocolate snowflakes 61
　wild birch bark 58
wild birch Christmas cake 58
Wimbledon tennis towers 129
winter crystals 150
wooden skewers 8

Acknowledgements

A huge thank you to Giuseppe for putting up with the chaos in the kitchen – not even the walls of cake boxes, mountains of ingredients bags and sprinkle-scattered work surfaces made your support waver. Your never-ending encouragement and faith in me is, well unbelievable.

Thank you to Adrian Lawrence for always going the extra mile. You embraced the fantasy cake and helped to give each design it's own little story with your amazing photography.

To Toni Kay, your creative vision for such a large project is inspiring, thank you for bringing to life my cakes throughout this book. I will never tire of turning the pages.

Thank you to Kate and Alice for your incredible juggling and organizational abilities – helping to make looming deadlines far less scary! And thank you for cutting and trimming with such a delicate hand!

To Jemima O'Lone, for your assistance your calm presence and cakey finesse in the kitchen is a real joy.

Thank you to Olivia Wardle for your beautiful prop styling and seemingly effortless way to 'just get it' – always finding the right props to echo and complement each cake design.

A massive thank you to mum for stepping in with the washing up when I'd used every utensil and the equipment cupboards were bare, re-assuring me it was all good. And that you actually like washing up when it's someone else's – that knowledge is now firmly in the pinny pocket!

And to dad, who whilst I developed recipes, took me by complete surprise and turned into a demon chameleon kitchen assistant, quietly helping out without me even realizing it. And both – thank you for making me the most awesome birthday cakes as a kid.

And to Julia Charles and Cindy Richards thank you for believing in me and giving me the creative freedom to allow my imagination to go a bit wild! I will never forget what a wonderful gift that is. You really have made a dream come true.